The Material of Poetry

Georgia Southern University

Jack N. and Addie D. Averitt Lecture Series

No. 13

Gerald L. Bruns

The Material of Poetry

Sketches for a

Philosophical Poetics

The University of Georgia Press

Athens and London

© 2005 by the University of Georgia Press
Athens, Georgia 30602
All rights reserved
Acknowledgments for previously published works and for tracks
contained on the accompanying CD appear on pages xviii–xxi,
which constitute an extension of the copyright page.
Set in Electra by BookComp
Printed and bound by Thomson-Shore
The paper in this book meets the guidelines for permanence
and durability of the Committee on Production Guidelines for
Book Longevity of the Council on Library Resources.

Printed in the United States of America
09 08 07 06 05   C   5 4 3 2 1

Library of Congress Cataloging-in-Publication Data
Bruns, Gerald L.
   The material of poetry : sketches for a philosophical poetics /
Gerald L. Bruns.
        p. cm. — (Georgia Southern University.
Jack N. and Addie D. Averitt lecture series ; no. 13)
   Includes bibliographical references and index.
   ISBN 0-8203-2701-8 (alk. paper)
1. Poetry.   2. Poetics.   I. Title.
II. Jack N. and Addie D. Averitt lecture series ; no. 13.
  PN1031.B83 2005
   808.1—dc22   2004014639

British Library Cataloging-in-Publication Data available

In Memory of Mentors and Friends

Joseph Schwartz

John and Peggy Gerber

Walter J. Ong, S.J.

Hugh Kenner

Contents

CD Tracks

1. Steve McCaffery, "Shamrock" (3:02)

2. Steve McCaffery, "First Random Chance Poem" (3:42)

3. John Cage, "Williams Mix" (4:23)

4. Steve McCaffery, "Mr. White in Panama" (2:17)

5. Christian Bök, "Der Ursonate" (20:23)

6. Jackson Mac Low and Anne Tardos, "Phoneme Dance for/from John Cage" (5:05)

7. Henri Chopin, "Sol Air" (9:50)

8. Henri Chopin, "Vibrespace" (8:51)

9. François Dufrêne, "Batteries Vocales" (2:15)

Illustrations

Foreword

The Averitt Lectures were established in 1990 through the generous gift of Dr. Jack N. Averitt and his wife, the late Addie D. Averitt, to bring to the campus of Georgia Southern University premiere scholars in the fields of history and literature. Each series of three lectures is intended for a heterogeneous audience of faculty, students, and the general public in accordance with the Averitts' long-standing commitment to enhancing the intellectual life of the university and the region of Georgia to which they have contributed so much.

We were honored to present Gerald L. Bruns as the Averitt lecturer in October 2003. Dr. Bruns is the William P. and Hazel B. White Professor of English at the University of Notre Dame. Dr. Bruns is interested in the relations between American and European literary cultures since the late nineteenth century, particularly in poetry, drama, and theater. His books include *Modern Poetry and the Idea of Language* (New Haven: Yale University Press, 1974), *Inventions: Writing, Textuality, and Understanding in Literary History* (Yale, 1982), *Heidegger's Estrangements: Language, Truth, and Poetry in the Later Writings* (Yale, 1989), *Hermeneutics, Ancient and Modern* (Yale, 1992), *Maurice Blanchot: The Refusal of Philosophy* (Baltimore: Johns Hopkins University Press, 1997), and *Tragic Thoughts at the End of Philosophy: Language, Literature, and Ethical Theory* (Evanston, Ill.: Northwestern University Press, 1999).

Dr. Bruns has won the National Endowment for the Humanities and Guggenheim Fellowships and has been a fellow at the Institute for Advanced Study at Hebrew University and at the Center for Advanced Study in the Behavioral Sciences at Stanford.

For his Averitt Lectures, Gerald Bruns chose as his subject recent avant-garde poetry. His lectures, titled *The Material of Poetry: Sketches for a Philosophical Poetics,* have now been expanded into this present volume, which, I believe, the reader will find both provocative and challenging.

As chair of the Averitt Lecture Series Committee, it was my honor to host Gerald Bruns during his stay on the Georgia Southern campus. I shall always remember his friendliness as much as the vigor and range of his conversation. Dr. Bruns's visit also marked the end of my tenure on the Averitt Lecture Series Committee, an involvement that brought me much satisfaction and pleasure. Now that my work has come to an end, I am pleased to thank one last time those colleagues and helpers whose dedication and commitment made the Averitt Lectures a success. First, I thank my friend and fellow worker, Dr. Dale Purvis, for her tireless attention to detail; for her sense of style, proportion, and beauty; and for helping me to laugh when I needed to regain my sense of humor. I thank my chair, Dr. Bruce Krajewski, for his enthusiastic support of the Averitt Lectures and for acquainting us with the work of Gerald Bruns. Thanks to Lanell VanLandingham and to our office assistants for cheerfully attending to many vital tasks. I express my appreciation to Helen Cannon, who knows better than anyone else how to show genuine southern hospitality to guests from all over the world. I thank Nicole Mitchell, director of the University of Georgia Press, for her unfailing support of the Averitt Lectures, and all of her staff who have produced such handsome books for us over the years. How can I forget Jane Kobres, assistant to the director at the University of Georgia Press, who walked with me through the thorns of trial to the soft grass of success? Jane, you know what I mean; I will never forget your help.

Finally, I speak for many people in thanking Dr. Jack Averitt for making these lectures, and this book, possible. The forward-thinking generosity shown by Dr. Averitt and his beloved wife has enriched the intellectual life of our university, our community, and, through books such as this one, the wide world beyond the campus and the region. Thank you, Jack. I believe your vision for the lectures and these books has been realized through the fine work of Gerald Bruns and his distinguished predecessors. It has been an honor for me to have shared your dream and made it real.

David L. Dudley
Chair, Averitt Lecture Series Committee

Acknowledgments

First of all I want to thank David Dudley and Dale Purvis for their invitation to deliver the thirteenth annual Jack N. and Addie D. Averitt Lectures at Georgia Southern University. It was wonderful to enjoy everyone's warm company and especially to spend time with Jack Averitt and to experience his remarkable gift of storytelling. I'm grateful to my friend Bruce Krajewski, chair of the Department of Literature and Philosophy at Georgia Southern, for his kindness, generosity, and undying passion for the writings of William James. Special thanks to Helen Cannon for her hospitality and excellent conversation.

I owe a great deal to my friends Marjorie Perloff and Steve Fredman, whose writings on modern and contemporary poetry are models of what the study of literature ought to be and who have made it extremely difficult for me to come up with any original ideas. Marjorie helped especially in reading a draft of this book, as did Steve McCaffery, whose poetry is one of the inspirations of my work in recent years. The intellectual companionship of Joe Buttigieg over the past twenty years has been of great importance to me. I'm also grateful to Anne Bruns Richardson, Andy Richardson, and Anne Montgomery for their help and guidance in putting this book together. My thanks to Wes Evard of the Office of Information Technologies at the University of Notre Dame for producing photographs of the illustrations.

And love to Nancy, Jacob, and James for looking after me.

Regarding the sound work contained on the CD that accompanies this book: Steve McCaffery's "Shamrock," "First Random Chance Poem," and "Mr. White in Panama" are reproduced by permission of Steve McCaffery and *Cabinet Magazine*. "Der Ursonate," by Kurt Schwitters, performed by Christian Bök, is reproduced by permission of *Cabinet Magazine* and Christian Bök. These recordings originally appeared on a CD accompanying *Cabinet Magazine* 1 (winter 2000/2001).

"Williams Mix" is reproduced by permission of the John Cage Trust and the C. F. Peters Corporation. Thanks especially to Laura Kuhn, director of the John Cage Trust, for her help and advice. The recording of "Williams Mix" that I have used is by Larry Austin and is taken from *Octo-Mixes, Larry Austin, Octophonic Computer Music, 1996–2001*, produced by Larry Austin and Joel Chadabe. Annotators: James Dashow and Larry Austin. Cover art: Jenette Dill. Score, page 5, and I Ching chart for John Cage's "Williams Mix," © 1960 by Henmar Press. Used by permission. CD design: Jenette Dill; (P) © 2001, EMF CD 039; CD available at http://www.cdemusic .org/; Electronic Music Foundation Ltd., 116 North Lake Avenue, Albany, NY 12206.

Jackson Mac Low's "Phoneme Dance for/from John Cage," performed by Jackson Mac Low and Anne Tardos, is reproduced by permission of Jackson Mac Low.

Henri Chopin's "Vibrespace" and "Sol Air" and François Dufrêne's "Batteries Vocales" are reproduced by permission of Henri Chopin. These recordings are available on *OU: Cinquème saison*, a four-disc anthology of audiopoems edited by Henri Chopin and published (Italy, 2002) by Henri Chopin and Alga Marghen.

Regarding the illustrations following page 51: "Der Ursonate," by Kurt Schwitters, is reprinted by permission of Jerome Rothenberg; "Phoneme Dance for/from John Cage" by permission of Jackson Mac Low; "Sol Air" by permission of Henri Chopin; "Carnival 1," "Carnival 2," "First Typestract," and "Bilingual Typestract" by permission of Steve McCaffery.

I'm grateful to Marvin Bell and Fred Courtright, The Permissions Company, for permission to reprint "About the Dead Man and Rigor Mortis" and "About the Dead Man and Government," from *The Book of the Dead Man* (Port Townsend: Copper Canyon Press, 1994), 41, 43; to

Charles Bernstein for permission to reprint passages from "Artifice of Absorption," from *A Poetics* (Cambridge: Harvard University Press, 1992), 9, 73; to Charles Bernstein and Fred Courtright, The Permissions Company, for permission to reprint "Emotions of Normal People," from *Dark City* (Los Angeles: Sun and Moon Press, 1994), 85–89; to Charles Bernstein and Fred Courtright, The Permissions Company, for permission to reprint "Sentences," from *Republics of Reality* (Los Angeles: Sun and Moon Press, 2000), 13–14; to John O'Brien and the Dalkey Archive Press for permission to reprint "Another Pebble" and "The Perfect World" from Gerald Burns's *Shorter Poems* (Normal, Ill.: Dalkey Archive Press, 1993), 55–56, 100–101; to Suhrkamp Verlag for permission to reprint Paul Celan's "ST," from Paul Celan, *Gesammelte Werke*, vol. 3 (Frankfurt: Suhrkamp Verlag, 1983), 136; to Clark Coolidge for permission to cite a passage from his *The Maintains* (Berkeley, Calif.: This Press, 1974), 1; to Willis Barnstone for permission to reprint Haroldo de Campos's "Alea I—Semantic Variations," which originally appeared in *Concrete Poetry*, edited by Mary Ellen Solt (Bloomington: Indiana University Press, 1968), 106; to Lyn Hejinian and Fred Courtright, The Permissions Company, for permission to reprint lines from *Writing as an Aid to Memory* (Los Angeles: Sun and Moon Press, 1996); to Lyn Hejinian and the University of California Press for permission to quote passages from *The Language of Inquiry* (Berkeley: University of California Press, 2000), copyright 2000 The Regents of the University of California; to Karen Mac Cormack and Coach House Books for permission to reprint "At Issue III" from *At Issue* (Toronto: Coach House Books, 2001), 9, 17; to Karen MacCormack for permission to reprint "Forgeries" from *Quill Driver* (Toronto: Nightwood Editions, 1989), 48; to Steve McCaffery and Coach House Books for permission to reprint "Hegel's Eyes," from *Seven Pages Missing*, vol. 1 (Toronto: Coach House Books, 2000), 292; to Steve McCaffery and Coach House Books for permission to cite the opening lines of "The Kommunist Manifesto," from *Seven Pages Missing*, vol. 2 (Toronto: Coach House Books, 2002), 171; to Editions Gallimard for permission to reprint Francis Ponge's "Le cageot," "Escargots," "Les plaisirs de la port," from *Le parti pris des choses, suive de Proêmes* (Paris: Gallimard, 1948), 171; to Wake Forest University Press

for permission to reprint the translations of Ponge's work, "The Crate,"
translated by Margaret Guiton, "The Pleasures of Doors," translated by
C. K. Williams, and "Snails," translated by C. K. Williams, from *Francis
Ponge: Selected Poems* (Winston-Salem, N.C.: Wake Forest University
Press, 1994), 17, 29, 43–44; to Editions Gallimard for permission to cite
lines from Ponge's "Le pré," from *Nouveau recueil* (Paris: Gallimard,
1948); to Serge Gavronsky for permission to cite lines from his translation of "Le pré," from *The Power of Language*, translated by Serge
Gavronsky (Berkeley: University of California Press, 1979), 77–78; to
New Directions Publishing Corporation for permission to reprint some
sixty lines of Cantos LXXIV and LXIX from *The Cantos of Ezra Pound*,
by Ezra Pound, copyright © 1934, 1937, 1940, 1948, 1956, 1962, 1963,
1966, and 1968 by Ezra Pound, used by permission of New Directions
Publishing Corporation; to Joan Retallack for permission to reprint "Afterrimages," from *Afterrimages*, © Joan Retallack 1995 (Hanover, N.H.:
Wesleyan University Press, 1995), 24; and to Joan Retallack and the pub-
lisher for "Scenes of Translation," from *How to Do Things with Words*
(Los Angeles: Sun and Moon Press, 1998), 43, copyright © 1998 by
Joan Retallack, reprinted with the permission of the author and pub-
lisher; to Peter Gizzi and the Estate of Jack Spicer for permission to
cite some lines from "After Lorca," from *The Collected Books of Jack
Spicer* (Santa Rosa, Calif.: Black Sparrow Press, 1989), 33–34; to Alfred
A. Knopf for permission to reprint Mark Strand's "Reading in Place"
from *The Continuous Life*, by Mark Strand, copyright © 1990 by Mark
Strand, used by permssion of Alfred A. Knopf, a division of Random
House, Inc.; to New Directions Publishing Corporation for permission
to quote six lines from *Paterson*, by William Carlos Williams, copyright
© 1946, 1948, 1949, 1951, 1958, by William Carlos Williams, used by
permission of New Directions Publishing Corporation, as well as a passage from "Pastoral," by William Carlos Williams, from *Collected Poems: 1909–1939*, vol. 1, copyright © 1938 by New Directions Publishing
Corp., used by permission of New Directions Publishing Corporation;
to Johns Hopkins University Press for Louis Zukofsky's "Lavender Cotton," from *Complete Short Poetry* (Baltimore: Johns Hopkins University
Press, 1991), 326, © 1991 Paul Zukofsky, reprinted with the permission

of The John Hopkins University Press; and to Wesleyan University·Press for permission to cite passages from Louis Zukofsky's essays collected in *Prepositions+* (Hanover, N.H.: Wesleyan University Press, 2000).

Every effort has been made to avoid any errors or omissions in the above list. Please advise if any corrections should be incorporated into future versions of this book.

The Material of Poetry

Introduction

An Apology for Poetry

When the dead man's writing is called "poetry," he laughs derisively.

The dead man sees no difference between a line and a sentence.

The dead man distributes definitions of poetry by reshaping the
concept. . . .

When the dead man writes a poem worth preserving, he immediately
burns it.

The dead man burns everything he writes, but pieces survive.

The fragment is more than the whole.

—Marvin Bell, *The Book of the Dead Man*

This book has a very traditional, even ancient, form, namely that of an *apology* for poetry. What sort of poetry? Much of what is now written and understood as poetry requires no apology because it is entirely within the frame of either the literary traditions that we study in school or the various social mechanisms that give writers public recognition—book awards, publication in upscale magazines, well-placed reviews—that sort of thing. What I am going to try to defend are poetic practices that have had and continue to have a conflicted relation to these established and establishing institutions. The difficulty that I face is that poetic practices are always shifting—not just changing but going underground, resurfacing, and doubling back, with radicals disguising themselves under familiar conventions, and vice versa. It is hard to engage the contemporary scene in art and poetry without missing something or without seeing something radical absorbed by forces of legitimation. The artist Lawrence Weiner once said something worth a good deal of thought: "When my work is assimilated into the art context, it will change something. I hope it won't be considered viable living art in ten years. . . . As what I do becomes art history the minute culture accepts it, so it stops being art."[1] Imagine a poem that ceases to be a poem by being accepted as such. This is one of the paradoxical possibilities that I want to analyze. I want to address poetries that (so it seems to me) still defeat our ideas and expectations of what poetry is—first, poetry whose language requires us to invent new concepts of what language is; second, sound poetry and its material counterpart, visual, or concrete, poetry; and third, poetry that seems to insert itself into the everyday world of banal objects, where it abides as one thing among others (a "found object").

No doubt, the history of poetry is made of heterogeneous, not to say rival and incompatible, practices, and as readers accommodate themselves to some traditions, others sneak up from behind. What I want to argue is that poetry is philosophically interesting when it is innovative not just in its practices but, before everything else, in its poetics (that is, in its concepts or theories of itself). Poetry is as much a conceptual art as it is an art of language.[2] Imagine, for example, an imaginary poem—Mallarmé's *Grand Œuvre*, Auden's "perfected poem which is not ours," Hart Crane's "single new *word*, never before spoken and impossible actually to enunciate."[3] The idea that the true poem is unwriteable has a distinguished history, at least since the Romantics, with their odes on dejection. However, at the other end of the scale, what if there were no criteria by which a piece of language, or a sound, or marks on a page, could be *excluded* as nonpoetry? An ideal poem out of reach is not a conceptual difficulty—poetic failure is one of poetry's richest themes. What is intellectually challenging is the possibility that anything, under certain conditions, may be made to count as a poem: The conceptual task is to spell out these enabling conditions.

Let me give a preview of what is to follow by first citing the Canadian poet Karen Mac Cormack, who has a poem that, as I read it, is neither (exactly) verse nor prose:

Forgeries

A parade anytime floats and south too an endangered species all listening in its dust. Caution mounts (reason given) ear the bell's heir. Waiting for crispness.

Delusion and the rain not talked about films on water and earth form ratio of how much read to when to write. Animal passed.

The working word. The use of another place is to go to. Baked goods the meaning of *rise*. To discuss glamour on this afternoon. Mileage hurtles by a reasonable man. The card game someone lasts through. The difference. "Wordlessly." "Without words." The sameness silenced.[4]

Karen Mac Cormack's sentences do not make the sentencelike sense of words that are trying to be definite statements about something. How the words of her text hang together is difficult to say, although on close reading one can see that, in certain unruly ways, hang together they do. Ears *are* bells' heirs, being recipients of ringing, even after the bells have ceased to sound. Meanwhile ears and heirs echo one another phonetically and, in a way, graphically as well. One waits for crispness while a toaster toasts toast. "The use of another place *is* to go to," because going to other places is what other places are for. "Baked goods the meaning of *rise*" means that, unleavened bread aside, there is no baking without dough rising. What is the difference between "Wordlessly" and "Without words"? A subtle one: "The sameness silenced." The conceptual irony of "Forgeries" is that, with apologies to grammatical form, the poem is made entirely of true statements. The question is, What makes one want to call the poem poetry? It suffers, after all, from a shortage of images, unless one counts "The card game someone lasts through"—the all-night poker game—as an image anyone can produce once the line has been contextualized. Perhaps "Forgeries" is not (just) a real poem but a text of forgeries (as poetic a word as ever existed): logical deformities taken as true.

My task in what follows is to give some reasons why we can—and should—read this writing, as well as much like it (and perhaps also unlike it), as poetry. Basically my approach is to apply to poetry the principle that Wittgenstein applied to things like games, numbers, meanings of words, and even philosophy itself. The principle is that the extension of any concept cannot be closed by a frontier.[5] What we take poetry to be cannot be exhausted by examples, because examples are always in excess of our experience and understanding. Anything goes, even if not everything is possible at once. Variations on this anarchic theme are played throughout this book, but my counsel is not to take fright, because, in a very conventional way, this anarchic theme defines the history of art and poetry the way the motto "the best theory so far" defines the history of physics—and perhaps, if Alasdair MacIntyre is right, the history of ethics as well.[6] Entering the history or, more accurately, the histories of poetry means being exposed to their multiple and unpredictable futures in which the forms of poetry are undergoing endless reconstruction. Hardly the time, in other words, for dogmatism or appeals to museum pieces; rather, the time is for strangeness, as in this recent poem by Joan Retallack, "Scenes of Translation":

LOCAL TRAVELLING	EXCURSIONS	SIGHT-SEEING

Trakl, I don't speak *Trakl*,   ¡Qué vista más bella!
Yo No Se Aleman* German   . . . .
n'either Ich-Ben 3PM   kay bees'-ta mas be'lya!

he says he can point /to/   O-O'LOGIST
the spot in the middle of the lake   ↑

where the elementary school
used to be   die Luft (über) (ist) alles
tragikomisch: fullesophagus   was bewundernswert
¡Absolutamente nadie!   was ihn völlig kalt ließ
No necesitan nada y   was sagen (ich will dir)
el anciano   corriendo   was brauchte er zu lügen

O-O Schmerz-Hund**   IS! a classic fable
that the thing   🖐 no hay de qué

ein eine of the sound of the pebble   cannot be spoken
[   ] kleine nicht [   ]   cannot be spoken[7]

**Trakl, Yo No Se Aleman*, Jorge Guitart, etc., et al., trans-fixed, J. R.[8]
**cf. "Schmerzgedichte," cf. also *42 Merzgedichte* (Jackson Mac Low)[9]

"Scenes of Translation" is a poem meant to be seen and heard as much as read. It is, as Marjorie Perloff says, an example of the *post-*

linearity of recent poetry, where the unit of verse is no longer the line but the word as such—or, more accurately, the word *and* the page, which is shaped or structured by typographical experiments that spoof our efforts of reading, the more so, in the case of "Scenes of Translation," because the poem originates in reading, being as it is a collage of found texts.[10] The poem is not closed to decipherment, but its intention might be to inspire speculation as to what it would be to translate familiar texts into unknown languages, mixed languages, or even nonlanguages. I must confess to a weakness for thought experiments provoked by questions like, What is a nonlanguage?

In this book I try to justify three theses. The first is that poetry is made of language but is not a use of it—that is, poetry is made of words but not of what we use words to produce: meanings, concepts, propositions, descriptions, narratives, expressions of feeling, and so on. The poetry I have in mind does not exclude these forms of usage—indeed, a poem may "exhibit" different kinds of meaning in self-conscious and even theatrical ways—but what the poem is, is not to be defined by these things. Poetry is language in excess of the functions of language (form doesn't follow function but confounds it). Poets in recent years have expressed this idea by criticizing and even repudiating words like "utilitarian," "communicative," "semantic," "transparency," "reference," "expression," and "narrative."[11] But what they mean by this is that poetry cannot be adequately conceptualized, valued, understood, or (much less) produced when in the service of the forms of discursive practice of which these terms are constitutive. The double bind occurs when we discover that much of contemporary poetry is in fact made of nonpoetic, everyday, socially and even intellectually distinctive forms of discourse. This is perhaps why conceptual nuances, if not casuistical distinctions, are what poetics is finally made of. It is why the problem of differentiating poetry from what it is not is, conceptually, of such philosophical importance. There is a sense in which poetry defeats philosophy if or when it cannot be properly identified, in which case poetry will have the last laugh on Plato and his exclusionary politics.

My second thesis contests the first by exceeding it. It is that poetry is not necessarily made of words but is rooted in, and in fact already fully formed by, sounds produced by the human voice (or voice and mouth), even when these sounds are modified electronically. What I'm aiming for here is a justification of *sound poetry*, where voice and mouth are no longer (just) instruments of speech or of musical sounds but become themselves the vehicles or, more exactly, events of art, if "art" is the word. Can there be such a thing as an art of *vociferation?* "Vociferation" is a term that has not received much theoretical investigation, perhaps because we associate it with garrulous old men. Vociferation means talking loudly, rapidly, annoyingly, endlessly, for its own sake; it also includes howling, grunting, choking, garbling. Vociferation means, basically, gratuitous action of the mouth, tongue, vocal cords—noise-making, for short, a species of agitation. Poetry in this event crosses over into the culture of performance art, whose aim or effect, as Arthur Danto has pointed out, is "disturbation."[12] Moreover, I want to investigate the internal kinship between sound and visual or concrete poetry. A poem made of letters or other orthographic symbols and seeking merely to form a spatial-visual structure may prove indecipherable but nevertheless, as the poet Charles Bernstein observed, "eminently performable."[13]

The first two chapters are meant to defend two (actually three) different conceptions of the materiality of poetry, by which I mean its irreducibility to functions of mediation, its semantic density or intransparency, and its corporeality and/or typographic mode of existence. There is, for example, warrant for thinking of sound poetry as a species of body art, where the body becomes the machine or vestibule of gratuitous expenditures of energy.[14] Having said this, I need to affirm, perhaps counterintuitively, that nowhere is there embedded in what I have to say a thesis or even a concession that this or any materialized poetry is meaningless. My argument is, rather, that the aim of the poetry or poetries that I want to examine is to expand our beliefs as to what is meaningful and to develop new ways of experiencing meaning. For most of us meaning just means familiarity or things belonging to a context. Meaning is what fits. But I think poetry exists to contest these routine textbook conceptions or stereotypes of meaning. What this contesting certainly might entail are experiences of language with potentially allergic side effects—laughter, anger, boredom, "disturbation"—all of which is frequently what happens on first (or even last) encountering sound poetry.

My third thesis is that, notwithstanding the arguments that I try to present in defense of the materiality of poetry, its irreducibility to serviceable forms of discourse, poetry does not occupy a realm of its own. It is not a purely differentiated species confined to a merely aesthetic, neutral, or disengaged dimension of human culture. Rather, precisely in virtue of its materiality, poetry enjoys a special ontological relation with ordinary things of the world. This is perhaps to put too high a price on the poetry in question, which in itself makes fairly modest claims, but which nevertheless, because of its preference for singularities or resistance to universals, arguably possesses an intimacy with mere things that defeats explanation. In Chekhov's *Three Sisters* a character worries about the meaning of life. She is answered by another character who says: "It's snowing outside. What's the meaning of that?" This seems coherent with a poem Jack Spicer desired to write:

> Dear Lorca, I would like to make poems out of real objects. The lemon to be a lemon that the reader could cut or squeeze or taste—a real lemon like a newspaper in a collage is a real newspaper. I would like the moon in my poems to be a real moon, one which could be suddenly covered with a cloud that has nothing to do with the poem—a moon utterly independent of images. The imagination pictures the real. I would like to point to the real, disclose it, to make a poem that has no sound in it but the pointing of a finger.[15]

Imagine a poem of pure extension, that is, one that does not mirror the world but contacts it as if language were a mode of touching and not just saying. This is not a mad idea. The French philosopher Emmanuel Levinas thinks of language not as a mode of cognition and representation but as a mode of proximity, sensibility, or contact, as if language were corporeal like skin. For Levinas, the proximity of other people is ethics. "The proximity of things," he says, "is poetry."[16] It is conceivable that poetry is as objective, and thus as resistant to interpretation, as any event of nature. If this is true, we need to develop concepts that help us to deal with this state of affairs. My proposal, as I indicate several times along the way, is that we should adopt an anthropological approach to poetry, meaning that in order to experience this (or any) poetry at all we have to integrate ourselves into the world or space in which the poetry is composed, become natives of this or that place, on the argument that what counts as poetry is internal to the social, historical, and cultural spaces in which it is written and read. I expect this is true even of a poem written in an imaginary language such as we find in a work by the Quebecois poet Claude Gauvreau, *Jappements à la lune*, which consists of eight short poems, one of which reads as follows:

> nrôm atila atiglagla glô émect tufachiraglau égondz-apanoir tufirupiplè-
> thatgouloumeirector ezdannz ezdoucrémouacptteu pif-legoulem ôz nionfan
> nimarulta apiviavovioc tutul latranerre dèg wobz choutss striglanima uculpt
> treflagamon.[17]

Of course, as Steve McCaffery indicates, Gauvreau's language is not, strictly speaking, imaginary. It is perhaps not a language at all but "an unmediated inscription of the materiality of the letter"—a poem in the manner of Isidore Isou and the *Lettristes*, who flourished in France in the 1950s and who argued that poems are to be made of letters and not of words and meanings, or of Iliazd (aka Ilia Zdanevich), a Russian avant-garde poet and painter who experimented with typographic constructions as performances in their own right and not simply as scripts and scores.[18] However, the question is whether one could learn how to produce a purely material inscription of letters according to Gauvreau's system, assuming there to be one. An imaginary (or, to be safe, a quasi) language is not necessarily a private language, and in any case Gauvreau's poem remains linguistical just to the extent that phonetic values remain attached to the letters so that the text could be performed as a sound poem or, as McCaffery does, studied as a species of surrealist imagery, with traces of representation and of a "differential operation" that makes meaning possible if not, in this instance, recognizable as such. As McCaffery says, "There is always the gesture towards familiar phonic patterns. The letter groupings often seem to serve as graphic *indications* not entirely contained within the category of 'meaning' but constantly suggesting it as a juxtaposed elsewhere. As such graphic indica-tional phenomena, the *Jappements* petition the semantic as a structural proximity that is never entirely reached. By preserving the *semblance* of words (i.e., a disposition, through intelligible spacing, to significance) the writing remains attached to the spectre of a semanticism."[19] The anthropological moral of the story is that it is very likely impossible for nonsemantic poetry to be merely unintelligible so long as we approach it with the kind of openness and responsibility that anthropologists bring to the strangeness of alien cultures.

1 Poetry as an Event of Language

The Conceptual Achievement of Contemporary Poetics

Beauty is beauty even when it is irritating.

—Gertrude Stein

Poetry scares me.

—Charles Bernstein

During the late 1970s and early 1980s a surprising number of English-speaking philosophers began taking a philosophical interest in literature. Some may remember Martha Nussbaum's argument that Henry James's novel *The Golden Bowl* is not just an illustration of something moral philosophers think about; it is itself a practice of philosophy because it gives us a thick description of a moral agent who acts rightly in a situation so complex that no set of moral principles could have guided anyone through it. Particular examples, not rules for every occasion, are really what moral philosophy is about. In a similar spirit Alasdair MacIntyre proposed that literary forms like the medieval quest-romance provide exemplary models of the good life because they show how pursuit of the good makes human life rationally coherent, and it is precisely by internalizing such narratives—living them—that we take on an identity in Aristotle's sense of *ethos* or moral character. Richard Rorty meanwhile thought that the greatest achievements of the European Enlightenment were not philosophical treatises that aim at the essence of things but novels that give us things in all their plurality and irreducible differences. Dickens trumps Heidegger and his "Being of beings" because he gets down to everyday details and gets them right. Arthur Danto thought that literature is philosophical in the same way possible-worlds theory is philosophical, even more so because literature gives us critical alternatives from which to judge and possibly change the world we actually inhabit. And so on, including Stanley Cavell's idea that the moral of modern skepticism, namely that our relation to the world and to others in it is not one of knowing but one of responsiveness and acceptance, is already fully articulated in Shakespeare's major tragedies.[1]

The common thread that ties these philosophers together is the assumption that what counts as literature is narrative. Each of them is a good cloth-coat Aristotelian for whom literature is made of character and action and is to be read as a plotted picture of how things are or could be—a theory that preserves Aristotle's view that diction or language, although in the service of narrative, is not essential to it.[2] This premium on narrative, with its corresponding bracketing or erasing of language, raises for me the question of what would happen if philosophers of this (mostly analytical) sort took an interest in poetry, especially if it is true, as poets have fairly consistently maintained, that in poetry language is not reducible to standard logical operations like telling a story. The question is doubly interesting, because, with perhaps the exception of Cavell, each of these philosophers seems a little suspicious of poetry— Rorty even thinks that it was Heidegger's interest in Hölderlin and Rilke, rather than in Rabelais or Cervantes, that proved to be his undoing, turning him from the down-to-earth author of *Being and Time* into an otherworldly "ascetic priest" who thought the Nazis were here to save us from modernity.[3]

Of course, one has to ask what a philosophical interest in poetry might look like, as well as what sort of poetry would inspire such interest. My idea is that what is *philosophically* interesting is a poem that is *not* self-evidently a poem but something that requires an argument, theory, or conceptual context as a condition of being experienced as a poem (or of being experienced at all), as if poetry were, as I think it is, a species of conceptual art, where the relation between theory and practice is a two-way street. In reading a poem, one might experience a theory of what poetry is. The point is that what requires no thought, what can be accepted without question—the chestnut, the museum piece—cannot be of much philosophical interest. A kind of oblivion hovers over "the canon."

As the British poet Allen Fisher has pointed out, poets do not mindlessly write poems; they develop (often under antithetical conditions) "project schemas" and "conceptual programs" that give their poems (even improvised or experimental ones) a kind of reason.[4] *What* kind of reason exactly? Almost certainly it is one that appears historically from below rather than one that descends transcendentally from above—and one that arrives from the future and dovetails unexpectedly with what comes down to us from the past. The point is that for philosophers to take an interest in poetry they might have to break away from what is universal, necessary, or legitimated by consensus to attend to what is local, contingent, and unheard of; philosophy would have to turn into poetics, a ground-level inquiry or argument as to what, in the face of rival and incompatible claims, counts as poetry. (It would have to become *modernist*.) The ancients, or some of them, thought of poetics as a branch of rhetoric that teaches a person how to write a poem; others—one might call them formalists—think of it as the formation of genre descriptions in answer to questions like, What is a lyric? As a historicist of an old-fashioned kind, I think of poetics as something closer to anthropological descriptions of strange practices and unnatural acts.[5]

Of course, our philosophers (not to say the rest of us) could, and perhaps do, take recreational, conservatory, or allegorical interests in poetry without undergoing an anthropological experience, much less any sort of conceptual crisis. After all, much of what is accepted as poetry today, or for the past two centuries, or even for the past two millennia, plays pretty much by Aristotle's rules. The canonical principle would be that poetry possesses, like all discourse, an inner logic and an "aboutness" (plot and *mimesis*). If for the ancients poetry was the versification of tradition or of religious and erotic *topoi*, for us moderns poetry is the versification of *experience* (allowing for several senses, not to mention objects, of the word "experience"). Academic quarrels about critical methods notwithstanding, the university study of poetry, such as it is, is not governed by concepts and examples much different from the criteria and models that underwrite such respectable institutions as *The Harvard Anthology of Contemporary American Poetry, Poetry: A Magazine of Verse, The New York Review of Books,* the poet laureateship of the United States, the Academy of American Poets, National Poetry Month, the Pulitzer Prize, and Garrison Keillor's *Writer's Almanac.* Ours is, being Western, an Aristotelian culture, where unity and coherence of form, clarity of meaning, and rhetorical accessibility are indispensable conditions of efficient coexistence. Much of modern and contemporary poetry remains more or less faithful to these conditions. Here, for example, is poet Mark Strand's theory:

> When I say "lyric poems," I mean poems that manifest musical properties, but are intended to be read or spoken, not sung. They are usually brief, rarely exceeding a page or two, and have about them a degree of emotional intensity, or an urgency that would account for their having been written at all. At their best, they represent the shadowy, often ephemeral motions of thought and feeling, and do so in ways that are clear and comprehensible. Not only do they fix in language what is often most elusive about our experience, but they convince us of its importance, even its truth. Of all literary genres, the lyric is the least changeable. Its themes are rooted in the continuity of human subjectivity and from antiquity have assumed a connection between privacy and universality.[6]

Strand has a recent poem about this kind of poetry, "Reading in Place":

Imagine a poem that starts with a couple
Looking into a valley, seeing their house, the lawn
Out back with its wooden chairs, its shady patches of green,
Its wooden fence, and beyond the fence the rippled silver sheen
Of the local pond, its far side a tangle of sumac, crimson
In the fading light. Now imagine someone reading the poem
And thinking, "I never guessed it would be like this,"
Then slipping it into the back of the book while the oblivious
Couple, feeling nothing is lost, not even the white

Streak of a flicker's tail that catches their eye, nor the slight
Toss of leaves in the wind, shift their gaze to the wooded dome
Of a nearby hill where the violet spread of dusk begins,
But the reader, out for a stroll in the autumn night, with all
The imprisoned sounds of nature dying around him, forgets
Not only the poem, but where he is, and thinks instead
Of a bleak Venetian mirror that hangs in a hall
By a curving stair, and how the stars in the sky's black glass
Sink down and the sea heaves them ashore like foam.
So much is adrift in the ever-opening rooms of elsewhere,
He cannot remember whose house it was, or when he was there.
Now imagine he sits years later under a lamp
And pulls a book from the shelf; the poem drops
To his lap. The couple are crossing the field
On their way home, still feeling that nothing is lost,
That they will continue to live harm-free, sealed
In the twilight's amber weather. But how will the reader know,
Especially now that he puts the poem, without looking,
Back in the book, the book where a poet stares at the sky
And says to a blank page, "Where, where in heaven am I?"[7]

One could imagine a philosopher of our designated stripe admiring this poem for its Aristotelian virtues, as well as for its neat holographic complexity—a poem about an imaginary poem about an ephemeral evening experience that exists nowhere except in the experience of an imaginary reader who in the end closes us up with an unwritten poem inside an imaginary book, perhaps the one Mallarmé imagined when he said famously, "all earthly existence must ultimately be contained in a book,"[8] all earthly existence, that is, save the poet, who has been translated into the empyrean as a condition of the poem's composition. The poem reminds us that no one should underestimate the importance or viability of a "poetry of experience"—a subject to which my mentor at the University of Virginia, Robert Langbaum, devoted a book that will never go out of date.[9] Poets like Elizabeth Bishop, Charles Simic, and Philip Levine come to mind.

I prefer Marvin Bell, particularly his recent "Dead Man Poems," which defeat a host of romantic stereotypes by forcing on us the existence of the poet as a geriatric case study who no longer experiences his body as a source of desire but now, Beckett-like, as a terminal fact of life. In fact the poems are pieces of necromancy in which the dead man ruminates on his posthumous condition, as well as on his historic past. Here is an excerpt from "About the Dead Man and Rigor Mortis":

> The dead man thinks his resolve has stiffened when the ground dries.
> Feeling the upward flow of moisture, the dead man thinks his resolve has stiffened.
> The dead man's will, will be done.
> The dead man's backbone stretches from rung to rung, from here to tomorrow, from a fabricated twinge to virtual agony.
> The dead man's disks along his spine are like stepping-stones across a lake, the doctor told him "jelly doughnuts" when they ruptured, this is better.
> The dead man's hernial groin is like a canvas bridge across a chasm, the doctor said "balloon" when they operated, this is better.[10]

Marvin Bell's poetry of experience in his dead-man poems is not what one would think of as *lyrical* experience. I think of his poems as *thought* experiences—experiences that are simultaneously mundane and impossible, and also unfailingly funny. (My students refer to Bell's poetry as "deadpan poems.") Here are the opening lines of "About the Dead Man and Government":

> Under Communism, the dead man's poems were passed around hand-to-hand.
> The dead man's poems were dog-eared, positively, under Communism.
> The dead man remembers Stalin finally strangling on verbs.
> The dead man's poems were mildewed from being hidden in basements under Fascism.
> Embedded in the dead man is a picture of Mussolini hanging from a noun.
> The dead man didn't know what to say first, after the oppression was lifted.[11]

In the dead man's poetry, language is lucid but (like life) lethal.

Poetry can also provide an experience of less than lucid language—an experience for which, in what is surely now *late* modernism, we never-theless still do not have a satisfactory theory.[12] Here, for example, are the opening lines of a poem by Clark Coolidge, *The Maintains:*

laurel ratio sharp or hard
instrumental triple to or fro
granule in award
one to whom is made
nave
bean
shin
spectacle
as the near wheel
of all subdue
a overhang
or bear over as a knot pass
the spread
that fair
the part
of the part plots
ending in for the most part bolts
as of wholes
golds
come to as risen divides[13]

The Maintains is a paratactic poem of some ninety-eight pages. Parataxis is a figure of speech in which the units of discourse are not integrated syntactically into a hierarchy but lie side by side the way they would in a cryptogram—"laurel ratio sharp or hard." In this poem the unit of discourse is not the line but the single word, or perhaps even the morpheme; but unlike the cryptogram these forms cannot be decoded into a message. The poet Charles Bernstein (speaking, disingenuously, for all of us) writes about the experience of reading this poem as follows: "I feel I need a meaning to accompany this surface of words, to reassure me that they are about something, mean something. I want a way of reading these words, a way of interpreting them, that yields a fact, a story, a statement to accompany this surface."[14] Our automatic reaction in reading is to try to map onto the poem an Aristotelian poetics ("fact, story, statement"), and naturally what we experience is the poem's refusal to be read in these terms. But it is not as if the poem were trying to be about something and failing.

What caused Coolidge to write this way? One could borrow a line from Stephen Dedalus: "History is to blame." Coolidge took his inspiration from a number of poets and artists like John Ashbery and John Cage who, during the 1950s, discovered in Gertrude Stein's writings an alternative poetics to the one that informed the work of the most widely read poets of the time—Wallace Stevens, Robert Lowell, Richard Wilbur. It was Gertrude Stein who, in *Tender Buttons*, perfected the paratactic mode of composition:

Colored Hats

Colored hats are necessary to show that curls are worn by an addition of blank spaces, this makes the difference between single lines and broad stomachs, the least thing is lightening, the least thing means a little flower and a big delay a big delay that makes more nurses than little women really little women. So clean is a light that nearly all of it shows pearls and little ways. A large hat is tall and me and all custard whole.[15]

The motto of art history is that anything is possible, but not everything is possible at every moment. Gertrude Stein made a certain impossible way of writing possible for poets like Coolidge, who was in turn one of the formative figures among a group of poets—sometimes, not without serious difficulty, called "language poets"—who began writing during the sixties and seventies just as narrative (the normative genre of "structuralist poetics") was reaching its cultural ascendancy and who turned against the logic or principle of integration on which narrative depends.[16] "Turned against" is perhaps too definite or limiting an expression, because these poets were at the same time reappropriating certain kinds of narrative (or, more accurately, novelistic) forms as a way of altering the tradition of lyric self-expression; but *anacoluthia*, the figure of speech that means "the want of grammar," describes economically the group's (early) poetic project of defamiliarizing language.[17] The idea was to try out different ways of freeing language from its cultural reduction to utilitarian systems for the standardization, commodification, and frictionless distribution of meanings, images, cultural forms, and even ordinary things of everyday life.[18] Like so much of what we now call "modernism," language poetry resisted what Max Weber called "the rationalization of the world," that is, the attempt to bring things and people under conceptual, instrumental, and bureaucratic control, making the world transparent to human consciousness and subject to human interests. For example, in his "Artifice of Absorption," Charles Bernstein thinks of poems this way:

> I would call them
> resistances—a dread,
> or refusal, of submission
> to a rule-governed wor(l)d,
> the inscription of a "regulated social order"
> into language[19]

The language poets, who adopted Gertrude Stein as their matriarch, began to treat language not (just) as an instrument of representation or expression but as a portion of reality to be investigated in all of its dimensions—linguistic, social, historical, literary, political, philosophical—and even (or especially) in its "ludic" or carnivalesque dimensions, the playful, gratuitous, libidinous, nonproductive expenditure of linguistic energy that at least since Aristophanes has always been a mark of literature. The Canadian poet Steve McCaffery thinks of "ludic" as synonymous with "poetic," and this excerpt from his poem in prose "Hegel's Eyes" shows what he means:

> We entered a city consisting entirely of grey thursday mornings. But the verb enter seems partly inappropriate plus appropriate itself seems wrong. So it would be wrong to say the city could be entered though all its thursdays are grey and though grey itself consists entirely of its mornings. Today then is the morning when the verb to enter will seem wrong. Today as the day plus all the inappropriate parts themselves that still seem proper.

So we can leave the city alone. Plus by ourselves. And having reached another city on a day like any other day we can stop to say we can drop in on
a day whose morning registers an off-white mood entirely. Plus we can say
we have entered a verb which seems wrong and wrong in the entirely correct
sense of wrong. Wrong being wrong and day being day. Hence tautological.
Plus inappropriate.[20]

McCaffery calls his writing "poetic research into the endless possibilities
of language," and his work is staggering in its range of experiments:
It includes sound and visual poetry, as well as texts that translate one
form of English into another—most famously McCaffery translates a
standard English translation of Karl Marx's *Communist Manifesto* into
the West Riding of Yorkshire dialect that he spoke as a child:

A spectre is haunting Europe—the spectre of communism. All the powers of
old Europe have entered into a holy alliance to exorcise this spectre: Pope and
Tsar, Metternich and Guizot, French Radicals and German police-spies.

Nah sithi, thuzzer booergy-mister mouchin un botherin awl oer place—
unnits booergy-mister uh kommunism. Allt gaffers errawl Ewerup's gorrawl
churchified t'bootitaht: thuzimmint vatty unt king unawl, unner jerry unner
frogunt froggy bothermekkers, unt jerry plain cloouz bobbiz.[21]

"Poetic research into the endless possibilities of language" means, anarchically, that *anything goes*. Nothing is forbidden or is to be stipulated
in advance: The principles, rules, methods, or practices of writing (the
"project schemas" and "conceptual programs") are to be invented as
you go and discarded upon use. "I have no steady poetics," McCaffery
notes in his "Poetics: A Statement," "no position or school that I defend, no fixist stance on art or anything else. I have a constant stream
of feelings and ideas that constantly change, modify and carry into action as techniques for living. What I try to do is understand this flux
and develop for myself a thoroughly nomadic consciousness; a mind
in constant movement through stoppings and starts, with the corollary
of a language art in permanent revolution, contradiction, paradox and
transform."[22] Coolidge takes it to the limit: "there are no rules. What I
think is that you start with materials. You start with matter, not rules."[23]

And the matter is language or, more exactly, words or, more exactly still, the material of words—the sounds of the voice and the letters of the alphabet, where the letters are experienced not only phonetically but also, as in visual poetry, as patterns of print or ink.

The word "matter" can and should be taken literally in all sorts of ways. Coolidge trained for a while as a geologist and has a passion for the mineral world (one of his collections of poems is titled *Geology*; another is *The Crystal Text*; still another is *Mine*, as in coal mine). And so he invites us to imagine the page as a space in which to place words like stones in a display case, each stone having its own properties to be closely examined and an uncanny ability to change its appearance when placed among stones of a different character.[24] In a talk titled "Arrangement," presented at the Naropa Institute for Poetics in 1978, Coolidge said that his intent is not to compose words into a poem—that is, it is not to integrate them into a normative semantic unit—but to arrange them on a neutral surface as if constructing a collage or wordscape.[25] "In the space my mind inhabits to write," Coolidge remarks in *Notebooks (1976–1982)*, a kind of *ars poetica*, "there seems no time."[26] So for him it is not necessary for words to hang together as they do in conventional structures like sentences, paragraphs, and narratives—or even lines of prosody—in which words are temporalized or disappear into an ensemble of relations. As the poet Barrett Watten notes, Coolidge's early syntax is spatial.[27] Coolidge, at this period, took "arrangement" to be an alternative to terms of art like "composition," "structure," and "form." In contrast to composition, structure, and form, arrangement tolerates sequences of words that might not go together, that resist integration, that insist on occupying their own independent space. (Coolidge asks us to hear the word "range" in "arrangement," as if it were not part of a whole, and moreover he asks us to think about the multiple senses of this word, taking it not as one word but as many, reading the word "arrangement" finally as an open-ended pun.) One of Coolidge's terms of art is "obdurate" (resistant, "sharp or hard"), a term frequently applied to rocks but that he applies to words. Barrett Watten says that Coolidge's words are "imponderables."[28] Note that the words in the title of Coolidge's poem are dissonant with respect to one another: *The*

Maintains. The one word turns the other into a noun, but the other resists because it is, after all, a verb. Its existence as a verb, therefore, is experienced differently from the way we would experience it if it were used correctly in a sentence like, "He maintains that *x* is *y*." And that seems to be the point of *The Maintains* as a poem: to decontextualize words so that we can experience them as such, not only in their function but also in their singularity and irreducibility, their *obduracy*, as well as in their relation to other words that happen to be in range morphemically and therefore even semantically (it's hard not to experience *Maintains* as a misprint of *mountains*). But we need to enlarge our concept of the semantic in order to understand what Coolidge is doing.

Coolidge was a close friend of Aram Saroyan, who composed one-word poems. As a poet, Coolidge was, at this time, austere, but not that austere. Recall some lines just cited:

> that fair
> the part
> of the part plots
> ending in for the most part bolts
> as of wholes
> golds
> come to as risen divides

In an essay on "How to Nonread," the antiparatactic language poet Gerald Burns says that the trouble with poems of this sort is that " 'reading' them means finding ways to make them interesting, to recover them from dullness."[29] But of course "finding interesting ways to read" is the philosophical challenge of paragrammatical poetry, as Burns well knows. I think it is possible to experience these words as something other than nonsense. It's hard to ignore the word "part," for example, which ranges through the stanza and through a range of senses: Each appearance of the word requires that we read it differently, hear a different idiom, keep different possibilities of meaning simultaneously in play. "[T]he part / of the part" might mean the division of it, where "ending" is the part of the plot that makes it whole or complete. Do we know what the word "part" means in the idiomatic expression "for the most part"? (Do we even hear or see it?) The word "bolts" is a sort of anagram of "plots"; it is also a word for exits or endings, as well as a word for thingamajigs that hold things together, like plots. In a paratactic poem, the displacement of syntax means that words can enter into all kinds of unpredictable semantic relations and evoke many possible contexts.[30] So the problem is arguably not one of nonsense but of too much sense, augmented or invigorated by alliteration, assonance, and echoes of all sorts ("bolts / wholes / golds"). *The poem forces us to expand our boundaries of what we think of as meaningful.* Over the course of ninety-eight pages it teaches us something about the limits of exegesis or about the shortfall in the way we are taught to read in school, where the rules of information theory are almost exclusively in force. Gerald Burns has a nice way of putting it: "Any poem teaches you how to read it. A long poem teaches you to live with it."[31] As noted earlier, poetry requires us to become anthropologists: We make sense of a poem not by the application of critical methods but by living with it until we are part of its world. Anthropologists like Clifford Geertz call this process "becoming real." We have to integrate ourselves into alternative poetic worlds and not restrict language to what seem to us self-evident poetic criteria.

Here is part of a poem by Lyn Hejinian, *Writing as an Aid to Memory:*

11.
                     nothing less is done in one year block
     cut it only in dark reduction
         how ness posites
   autobiography sees the world
    by early beginning with the top narrate
                much intention is retrospective and much
      extension is prospective
       for illusion of men can be so many scandals
               shifting quite but admirable victed
             sequences
    hoot random consciousness takes its chance
a narrow chance
         I can imagine boots as I imagine feet
             the sound for words makes me
             the digressions is a tender essential

In an essay titled "The Rejection of Closure," Hejinian distinguishes, as do many of her contemporaries, between closed texts and open ones. A closed text is one whose elements are fully integrated (no leftover parts) and that one reads as if converging on a single point; an open text is paratactic, made of gaps or cuts. For a closed text the serious problem is a word that is out of place or doesn't seem to fit; an open text meanwhile borders on disaster because, as Hejinian says, the problem is how "to prevent the work from disintegrating into its separate parts—scattering sentence-rubble haphazardly on the waste heap."[32] Paratactic poems destroy "aboutness" and thereby form, integrity, and ready-to-wear intelligibility. Repetition is one solution to this disintegrative problem: *Writing as an Aid to Memory* is a vast echo chamber whose lines and fragments resonate with the themes of writing and memory ("autobiography sees the world"), but the lines and fragments also echo one another. One word picks up on another (or on itself) in any number of unpredictable ways: The word "done" in the first line could mean either "accomplished" or "over and done with" (gone for good); "block" blocks the first line's passage to the second, while introducing the second line's glottal stoppages ("cut," "dark," "duct"); "block" could be a cutting block or what gets cut, like blocks of words or words themselves; "ness," "posites," and "victed" are pieces of cut words; "much intention is retrospective and much / extension is prospective" are, theoretically, true statements and, like "shifting . . . sequences" and "hoot random consciousness takes its chance," seem to reflect the poem's philosophy of composition. Are there grammatical mistakes in the last two lines cited, "the sound for words makes me" and "the digressions is a tender essential"? The words hang together semantically without the mediation of grammatical forms. The main point perhaps is that hearing relations is more productive than seeing them, supposing that we accept the ocularcentric argument that grammar and intelligibility are essentially modes of seeing.

But here is the difficulty: Can what I am doing with this poem be called *reading* it? Aristotelian exegesis seeks to fix meanings by working out the relation between parts and whole, text and context. Meaning just means belonging to a context (the old hermeneutical circle). Hejinian's idea is instead to turn meanings loose, leaving contexts open so that words are more like events to be performed than components of a structure. She writes: "Any reading of these [open] works is an improvisation; one moves through the work not in straight lines but in curves, swirls, and across intersections, to words that catch the eye or attract attention repeatedly."[33] So the idea is indeed to wonder, for example, what "the sound *for*," rather than "the sound *of*," a word might be and whether grammatical mistakes in a poem might have a semantic subtext. Wondering is itself an open form, like the question; Hejinian's poem doesn't let you into a declarative mood. It compels you to read constructively rather than consecutively.

For Hejinian, however, "open" means more than open ended, playful, aleatory, or nonlinear; it also means open to what is outside the poem. (Imagine a porous poem.) She writes: "The 'open text,' by definition, is open to the world and particularly to the reader. It invites participation, rejects the authority of the writer over the reader and thus, by analogy, the authority implicit in other (social, economic, cultural) hierarchies. It speaks for writing that is generative rather than directive. The writer relinquishes control and challenges authority as a principle and control as a motive. The 'open text' often emphasizes or foregrounds process, either the process of the original composition or of subsequent compositions by readers."[34] The open poem in this respect is a different poem each time it is read: If reading involves the improvisation of word connections beneath or beyond syntax, then there is no poem that one can step into twice. The open poem is a kind of low-tech hypertext. Imagine reading as a kind of performance art. But of course to imagine this we have to engage the poem as an event rather than simply as an object. And to imagine this we may have to change—change not just our concept of reading but our practice of it.

(Here, if I had space, I would discuss in more detail Hans-Georg Gadamer's aesthetics of participation, with its idea that the work of art is an event as well as an object, in which case the main question to ask about the work is not, "What is it?" or "What does it mean?" but "How does it occur?" The answer is that the work occurs in our encounter with it—that is, what is encountered is the coming into appearance of the work, which is not an event that merely reproduces an original production; it is the emergence of the original itself in an entirely new way. As Gadamer says, "presentation [*Darstellung*] is the mode of existence of the work of art."[35] That is, the being of the work consists in its being performed like a drama or played like a piece of music: "it is in the performance and only in it . . . that we encounter the work itself."[36] Or again: "the presentation or performance of a work of literature or music is something essential, and not incidental to it, for it merely completes what the works of art already are—the being there of what is presented in them."[37] Performance is not something added to the work or a rendition or version of it; it is the work itself. Gadamer goes so far as to say that "however much [the work] is transformed or distorted in being presented, it still remains itself. . . . Every repetition is as original as the work itself."[38] The work itself exists in no other way. Its coming into appearance is its mode of being.)

However, what does Hejinian mean when she says that the poem is open to the *world*? "World" in what sense? In "If Written is Writing," an essay composed in the same year as *Writing as an Aid to Memory*, Hejinian made the obscure statement that in her writing "the text is anterior to the composition, though the composition be interior to the text."[39] She seems to mean by this that language is not inside the poet as an innate grammar for generating sentences; rather, the poet is inside of language—inside, moreover, not as in a control center but as in an environment, one that is social and pragmatic rather than simply linguistic in the systematic, deep-structured, rule-governed Chomskyan sense. The "anterior text" within which composition takes place is *parole*, the singular speech act, not *langue*, the linguistic system that we use to speak. The poet in this event does not so much *use* language as interact with uses of it, playing these uses by ear in the literal sense that the poet's position with respect to language is no longer simply that of the speaking subject but also, and perhaps mainly, that of one who *listens*. (Hejinian's poetics reminds us that, in contrast to the egocentric models proposed by logic, linguistics, and the philosophy of language, we experience very little of language when merely speaking it.) Hejinian writes: "One locates in the interior texture of such language as is the person composing from it, personal and inclusive but not necessarily self-revelatory—in fact, now, seldom so: through improvisatory techniques building on the suggestions made by language itself—on patterns which are ideas and corresponding behavior or relevant quirks. This becomes an addictive motion—but not incorrect, despite such distortion, concentration, condensation, deconstruction, and digressions that association by, for example, pun and etymology provide; an allusive psycho-linguism."[40] So poetry is as much a response to language—a citation and appropriation of it—as it is a form of lyric expression. The lyric subject is folded into language, which is no longer, strictly speaking, a form of mediation but a material reality out of which the poem forms itself.[41]

Or, to put it differently, imagine poetry as an absorption of the languages in which it is socially, historically, and culturally immersed. Charles Bernstein writes: "The social grounding of poetry cannot be evaded by recourse to a purely intellectual idea of the materiality of language since the materiality of language is in the first instance a social materiality."[42] A purely intellectual idea of the materiality of language might be one like Roman Jakobson's formalist notion that poetry foregrounds the rhetorical features of language—schemes and tropes (isomorphism, metaphor, and so on). The social materiality of language, by contrast, is not something formal or linguistic but something heard and also quite often tuned out. For example, an early poem of Bernstein's, "Sentences," is made entirely of ordinary sentences:

> It's an automatic thing. It doesn't require any thought. It's a parade in and out.
> It has its ups and downs.
> It doesn't affect me one way or another.
> * * *
> It sort of comes to you. I never look at it. The touch. My hands fit. It's the feel. I just look at them.
> * * *
> It'll sound terrible. It's true. It's nothing really. I like to fuss. I sit and relax and read, take a bath, have my ice cream. I fill the day.
>
> You look around. You hear things. Sometimes you daydream you're really somebody special. It's the sort of thing you do.

I could never converse with anyone about it.

It would drive me nuts. It would drive me wild. I know I'm needed. I think a lot. I have very simple pleasures. I'm not a deep reader. I can't understand a lot of things. I'm looking forward to it.

* * *

I always have a hard time saying it. It feels too personal. It seems inconsequential. It keeps me from knowing what to do.[43]

This is also a paratactic poem. Its sentences do not (quite) form a context. One reason they do not is that the poem's subject, what it is about, is illusory—the poem is built around an "it" that has no referent, rather like the diathetical "it" in "It is raining," where the verb "to rain" can only be articulated in what grammarians call "the middle voice" between active and passive, or between transitive and intransitive, constructions. The speaker of the poem occupies this same neutral space: It is a voice made of *found* language, and yet, for all of that, it acquires a certain personality as the poem develops. In truth the poem is a parody of the confessional lyric in which the poet can't quite put *it* into words. So on several readings the poem can be said to come together, in its way, after all.

Bernstein's poetry is difficult not because it is obscure in the way poetry often is (sheer density of language) but because it is rooted in parody, quotation, mimicry, and pastiche—and also in what performance artists call "breaking the frame": "What I like in poems," Bernstein says, "is encountering the unexpected and I enjoy not knowing where I am or what comes next. Which means I try to derail trains of thought as much as follow them; what you get is a mix of different types of language pieced together as in a mosaic—very 'poetic' diction next to something that sounds overheard, intimate address next to philosophical imperatives, plus a mix of would-be proverbs, slogans, jingles, nursery rhymes, songs. I love to transform idioms as much as traditional metrics."[44] The poem "Emotions of Normal People" (from *Dark City*) is an example of such a mosaic of social idioms, this time of the languages of an urban, upscale, commercial, electronic culture; it begins as follows:

With high expectations, you plug

Into your board & power up. The

Odds are shifted heavily in your

Favor as your logic simulator comes

On-screen.

The poem continues through fifty more lines of similar digital diction, which are followed without warning by a thank-you note (in a different typeface):

Dear Fran & Don,

Thanks so much for
dinner last night. You two
are terrific—we knew that about
you, Fran, but, Don—we don't
meet rocket engineers such as
yourself very often and so
meeting you was a special treat!
Next time—our little
Italian restaurant!

Warm Regards,

Scott & Linda

This in turn is followed by appropriations of the language of Wall Street and advertising:

Suddenly, in spite of
worrisome statistics that had unnerved
the Street, we
developed conviction and acted on it. Aside
from the arbs

and the rumor mill, the major trend remains up regardless of
street noise.
The liquidity is there, so any catalyst
should hasten the major direction. The market's internal technical condition is far from
overbought, which leaves
room to rally back to October's
2500.

I think our big problem is inhibiting post-normalization.

Success demands getting more from available space, taking efficiency to ex-
tremes, paying less for improved performance. Moreover, 2440 sacrifices none
of 2430A's performance.

Intuitive user interfaces provide only part of the road map out of the dark
ages.

We've made debugging easier with differential nonlinearity, monolithic
time-delay generators, and remote-error sensing terminals (RESTS). Yet, we
still face a severe memory shortage and rather than resolve the problem we're
buying our way out of it. We need a tariff on cheap foreign-made memory
so we can regroup our own. The current controversy, however, stems from
the attempts of several vendors to control the marketplace by promoting
standards that especially benefit their computing architecture.[45]

The poem continues through a dozen more styles, voices, and satirical
turns, including an ad aimed at poets: "A 1985 survey shows that 23.3 per-
cent of all writers write poetry—that's 2,180,000 people who are writing
poetry and want to get published. *2004 Poet's Market* contains current,
accurate, and complete information to help poets do just that."[46] (Compare Bernstein's lines to an actual recent blurb for *Poet's Market:* "GET
YOUR POETRY PUBLISHED! Poetry brings words to life with truth
and passion unequaled by ordinary fiction. It awakens the senses, evokes
powerful moods and moments in time. Get your poetry published with
2003 Poet's Market! It helps define and direct your efforts with listings
for more than 1,800 book, journal and magazine publishers and editors.

You'll also find information on grants, conferences, workshops, contests and more. Using easy, quick-reference symbols and indexes, you'll pinpoint the most promising opportunities for your work.")[47]

Recall the idea of the Russian critic Mikhail Bakhtin that language is not a formal system, except in theory or in school; in reality it is a *heteroglossia* of social languages, a "Tower of Babel" mixing of vocabularies, ways of speaking, "verbal-ideological" attitudes, regional dialects, institutional jargons, generational polyglots, buzz words, clichés, sound bites, and idiolects. Interestingly, Bakhtin thinks that the language of the novel is structured like a "social heteroglossia," whereas the language of the lyric is "a unitary, monologically sealed-off utterance," the product of the unique, private, expressive voice of the poet.[48] (Mark Strand's poem, cited earlier, conforms exactly to Bakhtin's theory of the lyric.) Bernstein wants to turn Bakhtin's idea inside out. He thinks that lyric poetry (as well as philosophy and literary criticism) suffers from "tone lock,"[49] that is, a generic monotone and uniformity of surface in which everyone, poets and professors, sounds alike. In an early essay, "Semblance," Bernstein writes:

> My interest in not conceptualizing the field of the poem as a unitary plane, and so also not using overall structural programs: that any prior principle of composition violates the priority I want to give to the inherence of surface, to the total necessity in the durational space of the poem for every moment to *count*. The moment not subsumed into a schematic structure, hence instance of it, but at every juncture creating (synthesizing) the structure. So not to have the work resolve at the level of the 'field' if this is to mean a uniplanar surface within which the poem operates. . . . Textures, vocabularies, discourses, constructivist modes of radically different character are not integrated into a field as part of a predetermined planar architecture; the gaps and jumps compose a space within shifting parameters, types, and styles of discourse constantly crisscrossing, interacting, creating new gels.[50]

The poem, for Bernstein, is not "a unitary, monologically sealed-off utterance," not a hermetic work of art occupying its own differentiated aesthetic space, but a derivation of social discourse, a staging of social reality that works like Bertolt Brecht's *Verfremdungseffekt:* Instead of being transported imaginatively or vicariously to another world, we are exposed critically to our own social environment. Bernstein's poetry *theatricalizes* the languages of everyday life, including the contexts in which these languages are used. It is true that the word "theatrical" is a two-edged sword. For many it is an anaesthetic term, synonymous with "fake." But "theatrical" also entails the phenomenological sense of making reality visible, palpable, and unavoidable through forms of hyperbole: Theatricality is the enemy of naturalization, normalization, standardization, routinization, and obliviousness. The poet Rachel Blau DuPlessis says that "The language of poetry is the language of anything," but in the poem "the language of anything" performs differently because it is literally "performing itself" and no longer simply functioning toward an end.[51]

I come round to the concepts of theatricality and performance by design, because in the second chapter I discuss, and try to defend, the contemporary practice of poetry as a performance art in its most theatrical and certainly most difficult form, namely sound poetry and varieties of acoustical art in which poetry ceases to be a genre distinction and becomes something like a limit-experience, an event that shuts down, or even breaks down, the cognitive mechanisms or defenses by which we process or filter our experiences. More than this, one might think of sound poetry as a surrealist or existentialist art of extreme situations whose aim, or anyhow whose effect, is to set a limit on, or pose the question of, what can be philosophically justified, which is to say given a reason. The same, as we shall also see, is true of poetry whose typographical arrangements condense the alphabet (or other orthographical symbols) into spatial and visual constructions that are sometimes readable, as in this portion of Joan Retallack's "Afterrimages"—

text breaks into architecture of page
floating Figs
scholar riding in Capital C

St. Cuthburt *all' curyouste he refused*
curiositas (*curo*, to care), Medieval sin

this is not to imply that we are any better

off

[................*fed*...] [....*re*........*piy*.... ....*erg*.......]

the dynamics of the picture forced him
to show roundness as a square

....

                               tect

                    Cap

               all

          to

off[52]

—and sometimes not.

"Afterrimages" is a poem of thirty texts, each of which "breaks into the architecture of the page," interrupting its smooth surface with sentence fragments, broken words, falling letters, lines, dots, and deletions of spaces between words, not to mention citations from texts both ancient and modern, including contemporary buzzwords. It is as if typographical variables had been set in motion with nothing to restrain them. The poem is actually an example of a "saturated phenomenon," a term phenomenologist Jean-Luc Marion coined to refer to experiences in excess of the concepts that make our intuitions of phenomena intelligible as intentional objects or significations.[53] Afterimages, the haphazard formations of light that we continue to see after we close our eyes, are elementary forms of such phenomena, but so are mere noises, mystical experiences as conceptualized in negative theology, and, as Marion has shown, a good deal of contemporary art, with its power to defeat every form of intentionality.[54] Arguably, sound and visual poetry are not as exceptional as we might think. Our experience of them is irreducible, unsettled, and unsettling, but hardly impoverished. On the contrary, as the term "saturation" implies, such poetry leaves us with too much rather than too little to comprehend: Our senses are overloaded by what is given to them. My thought is that we should resist the temptation to save ourselves by turning away and tuning out. Rather the challenge is to investigate these extreme forms of poetry and to develop contexts and concepts that will clarify them.

2 The Transcendence of Words

A Short Defense of (Sound) Poetry

It's all

in the sound.

—William Carlos Williams, "The Poem"

Let your ears send a

message of surprise or complexity.

—John Cage

It is sound more so than meaning binds

the body to language.

—Steve McCaffery

[Play Steve McCaffery's "Shamrock"]

In recent years I've become interested in certain connections between poetry and ethics. Perhaps I should say, between borderline, or limit-cases, of poetry and ethics. By "poetry" I mean particularly the work of the language poets but also the writings of many others (the poet John Ashbery, the avant-garde musician John Cage, the intermedia artist Dick Higgins, the philosopher-novelist William Gass)—those who see themselves as having, among other things, a strong allegiance to the writings of Gertrude Stein. These writers do not hesitate to explore and expand what Steve McCaffery calls the *protosemantic* dimensions of language—language on the hither side, the material or corporeal side, of our uses of it.[1] Moreover, they try to conceptualize these dimensions in ways that defeat our ideas of what poetry is.

By "ethics" I mean what the French philosopher Emmanuel Levinas means when he rejects the idea that "ethical" means fidelity to principles and rules or to concepts of the good, the right, and the just. Philosophical tradition (Aristotle, Kant) takes ethics to mean acting in accord with the legislation of reason or its equivalent: divine commands, moral traditions, or moral communities such as Alasdair MacIntyre understands them—ways of living that can be justified, if not on universal grounds, then historically as the best so far by critical comparison with others.[2] For Levinas, however, ethics has to do with the untheorizable *claim* that other people have on us. This is a claim that cannot be traced back to a reason or an order of things. My responsibility for the other—for the good of others—is *anarchic* in the etymological sense of being on the hither side of any principle (*arche*) that would justify me in advance, say a law or prior agreement or proviso that would rationalize my action (or nonaction) and thus place me above reproach. Levinasian ethics is, famously, Jewish rather than Greek, meaning that election trumps decision. In my responsibility for the good of the other I am like the biblical prophet who has been summoned out of my house and made answerable to and for the other. As an ethical subject I am no longer a cognitive agent exercising control under the safety of criteria, determining my own future, securing my interests. Rather as a subject I have been turned inside out and exposed to the other with nothing to fall back on that will exempt me from my responsibility. As Levinas says, "The word *I* means *here I am* [*me voici*], answering for everything and for everyone."[3] I exist in the accusative, not in the nominative case. As an ethical subject I am more skin than spirit, more passive (as Levinas likes to say) than all passivity. I am a sensible egoless *me* to whom the other happens. What kind of trauma is this—to cease being an ego? The figure of the scapegoat comes to mind.

Scapegoats aside, my thought has been that the kind of *reversal of subjectivity* that Levinas describes is analogous to the reversal that William Carlos Williams had in mind when he said, evidently under Marcel Duchamp's inspiration, that the poet's relation to language is one of listening or hearing and not just speaking or writing.[4] This fact opens up the possibility that a poem might be found rather than made, "set down as heard," as Williams puts it, rather than unfolded from somewhere inside the poet.[5] Imagine a poetry that, anarchically, just happens to a piece of language. This would mean that what poetry *is* cannot be settled in advance by principles, rules, traditions, or any sort of formal description unless of course we radically historicize these things, arguing that all theory is local and contingent, like Williams's assertion in *Kora in Hell* that "A poem can be made of anything," even newspaper clippings.[6] In fact, this anarchic, nominalist principle—call it the "unprincipled principle"—seems to be the watchword for much modern and contemporary poetry and art, both in North America and elsewhere, where the object is to keep open and even confound the question of what counts as poetry. I should add, as a sociological observation, that *resistance* to this anarchism and nominalism—this repudiation of universals or of steadfast criteria—has in recent years become one of the major projects of academic literary study.[7] No doubt this is because nominalism raises havoc with the formations of the canon, not to mention the syllabus or indeed the professional standing of those who write about poetry.

I agree that Williams would not have recognized himself in Levinas. However, the priority of hearing and listening over speaking and writing does make poetry, whatever else it might or might not be, a mode of *responsibility*, taking this word, as Levinas does, in its literal sense of responsiveness and receptivity, as well as in its ethical sense of answerability. That poetry is not assertive but receptive is an old idea; however, here it would be useful to gloss this concept with Stanley Cavell's Levinas-like argument (developed in his writings on Thoreau and Emerson) that our relation to the world, and to others in it, is not one of knowing—knowing as objectification or conceptual determination—but one of acknowledgment and acceptance, being open and responsive to people and to things rather than trying to get a grip on them.[8] Responsiveness to others and to things *in their irreducible singularity* calls for an intimacy that cognition rules out. The "I" or "me" in responsibility is in the unabstracted, undetached condition of nonindifference. Levinas calls this condition "proximity" and also "sensibility," where we exist in the mode of being touched rather than in the cognitive mode of grasping or appropriation.[9] Hearing or listening is perhaps the most inescapable way of dwelling in this anarchic condition.

Here I mean "anarchic" in the following way: Listening involves a form of subjectivity—indeed a kind of experience—different from seeing; it implies or entails a porous, as against a self-contained, mode of being, and it also implies a different world from the one that seeing, perception, observation, or conceptualization constructs or projects onto the screen of consciousness. In an essay on "The Transcendence of Words," Levinas says, "To see is to be in a world that is entirely *here* and self-sufficient."[10] Sound, however, undoes this state of self-sufficiency and contentment—and it is important to know that Levinas is thinking of the sounds of *words* rather than, say, *musicalized* or *harmonized* sounds. Specifically, he is thinking of *voiced* sounds in which sound is no longer a semantic medium or the embodiment of aesthetic form but rather a mode of sensibility *irreducible* to vision, comprehension, or containment within categories.

The "transcendence of words" means that through their sounds words are in excess of their functions of signification, conceptualization, narration, context formation, world-making, and so on. This would mean, as against certain simplified versions of deconstruction, that written words are more logocentric than spoken sounds: Spoken sounds are, as Derrida would say, older than the *logos* of words; sounds erase signs. Sounds overload the functions of language. They destabilize structures. To be sure, that Levinas should speak of the transcendence of words at all is a little surprising because "transcendence" is a word that he reserves for the other (*Autrui*), that is, the human person whose otherness consists precisely in being outside my grasp, refractory to my categories, emphatically not an object of my cognition, representation, or conceptual control; in other words, outside the world in which things are objects subordinate to my interests. Transcendence is a mode of radical exteriority, an outside that defines the limit of my power, ability, and activity. What Levinas proposes here is a link between the alterity of sound and the alterity of the human being. In their exteriority, both sound and the other call me into question as a cognitive subject, an *ego cogito* who commands or governs a view of things. Sound puts me back on earth, in a condition of finitude.

Levinas writes: "In sound, and in the consciousness termed hearing, there is in fact a break with the self-complete world of vision. In its entirety, sound is a ringing, clanging scandal. Whereas, in vision, form is wedded to content in such a way as to appease it, in sound the perceptible quality overflows so that form can no longer contain its content. A real rent is produced in the world, through which the world that is *here* prolongs a dimension that cannot be converted into vision."[11] A just and rational order of things, a fully integrated and harmonious world, would be completely silent. Such a world would tolerate little more than contemplation as a form of life: Its music would be a music of the spheres that only the most austere or bodiless ascetic could hear. Plato's Republic evacuates its poets not just because they traffic in images but because they are noisy and heterogeneous, not to say schizophrenic, making the soul's silent dialogue with itself, and thus self-knowledge, impossible (see Plato's first account of *mimesis* in book 2 of *The Republic* and Eric Havelock's *Preface to Plato*, on the psychology of the poetic performance in ancient Greece). Sound *decomposes* the self-identity of the subject, a self-identity that is the first principle of rationality. Sound is invasive; ears are porous in a way that eyes are not. Sound fills the subject with foreign material, driving the subject out of itself, whereas sight keeps things at a distance and in perspective. Sound is Dionysian; sight is Apollonian. Sight integrates not only what it sees but also the subject of seeing itself: Having a point of view is what makes us whole, self-identical, self-possessed, detached, autonomous, and impervious. Sound meanwhile makes one ecstatic in the nature of the case. It transforms the *I* of cognition and representation into the *me* whose existence is exposed and vulnerable. Sound bleeds the self.

Here we have then the beginnings of a conceptual context in which to think about, and perhaps even to experience in a *nonallergic* way, such a difficult thing as *sound poetry*, which includes audio or acoustical poetry (that is, poetry in which sounds of the voice and mouth are technologically modified), as well as ethnopoetics, word jazz, radio art (*hörspiele* or ear-plays), and other forms of aural or sonic performance, like Valère Novarina's "theater of the ears," in which the actor uses his or her body (with *all* of its orifices) as a medium for sound production rather than for the articulation of meanings.[12] To my mind sound poetry constitutes the most difficult and imponderable form of art in our culture. (It is without question the most underresearched form of modernist or contemporary art.) For me this means that we have a kind of anthropological obligation—and, in the Levinasian sense, an ethical obligation—to make sense of it.

[Play Steve McCaffery's "First Random Chance Poem"]

How are we to respond to this work (or event), with its ludic noises and repeated invocation of "Julian Dowager"? My approach is not only conceptual and theatrical but also, I have to confess, insufficiently analytical: I haven't figured out yet how to close-read a sound poem (except by cheating: find the "score" of the poem and read *that*). So I approach it first as a species of conceptual art and then as a kind of performance or even body art. In fact, concept and performance (the publication, staging, or exhibition of art) tend to be interdependent.[13] (Conceptualization is a species of framing or foregrounding; it dramatizes its content.) Two theses form the context I've been trying to construct. One is that there is an internal link between sound and the displacement of the ego from its presidential status as a logical subject exercising conceptual control over whatever it experiences. Moreover, there is a kinship here with the Objectivist tradition in American poetry, in which the poet's ego, as Louis Zukofsky expresses it, ceases to be "predatory" in relation to things such as sounds. "It is possible in imagination," writes Zukofsky, "to divorce speech of all graphic elements, to let it become a movement of sounds. It is this musical horizon of poetry (which incidentally poems perhaps never reach) that permits anybody who does not know Greek to listen and get something out of the poetry of Homer: to 'tune in' to the human tradition, to its voice which has developed among the sounds of natural things."[14]

The second thesis complements this idea: Namely, sound as such has a claim on our capacity for listening and responsiveness that is analogous to—has the force of—the ethical claim that other people have on us. This second thesis is consistent with many of John Cage's writings, because Cage's position was always that our responsibility for sounds corresponds to our responsibility for others—and vice versa—the idea being that our disposition toward the world should be one of listening rather than one of command and control. "Giving up control so that sounds can be sounds" is the first principle—a decidedly *unprincipled* principle—of Cage's aesthetics.[15] This principle underwrites the composition of Cage's famous "4'33"," a work in three movements in which a pianist sits at his instrument for four minutes, thirty-three seconds, timing the duration of the movements but not playing a note. However, there is no silence. The music consists of the sounds that are allowed to exist in the absence of the music. And so one hears, as I do, for example, a ringing in the ears, indeed a collage of several ringings, roarings, and swishings humming simultaneously (a condition known as tinnitus). Cage's argument is that giving up control of sounds does not mean giving up responsibility for them. One is not merely passive with respect to sound. As he says, "sounds, when allowed to be themselves, do not require that those who hear them do so unfeelingly. The opposite is what is meant by response ability" (S10).

Of course, here the prudent among us would hesitate. *What counts as sound?* Levinas has in mind the sounds of the voice and, more specifically, the sounds of spoken words. I think that Levinas has a biblical, specifically prophetic, conception of sound. He writes: "The sounds and noises of nature are failed words. To really hear a sound, we need to hear a word. Pure sound is the word."[16] Hearing for Levinas is an epiphanic event, perhaps even a hierophany, or at least the echo of a transcendent intervention. Sound is not a distraction but an imposition that requires us to respond; all sound is structured as a calling. To hear a sound is to be summoned like Abraham and Moses. Every sound is an emanation of the voice of God. God is meant to be heard, but not seen.

Cage's ear, by contrast, is that of a Zen Buddhist (which is what Cage was, if mainly after his own fashion). Cage's project was to emancipate music from its confinement to sounds made by instruments invented in the eighteenth and nineteenth centuries. By the time of his 1937 essay "The Future of Music: A Credo," Cage had abandoned the distinction between musical and nonmusical sounds (or "noise," for short). The point of this iconoclasm was to liberate sounds (and the ears that hear them) from the canonical history of classical music. In a 1957 essay, "Experimental Music," Cage describes two ways in which this liberation of sound can take place. One way is technological, which is to say by way of experiments with, among other things, electronic innovations like magnetic tape. Cage's piece "Williams Mix" would be a good example of this approach.

[Play John Cage's "Williams Mix."]

The other way is to become a listener, turning "in the direction of [sounds] one does not intend" (S8). In music, Cage says, "nothing takes place but sounds: those that are notated and those that are not. Those that are not notated appear in the written music as silences, opening the doors of the music to the sounds that happen to be in the environment" (S7–8). In other words, composers have a choice of methods: a Western way, through technological experiment, and an Eastern way, through the renunciation of intention and the elimination of one's ego, which means the opening up of one's subjectivity to the alterity of the world. Cage puts it this way: "If [the composer] does not wish to give up his attempts to control sound, he may complicate his musical technique towards an approximation of the new possibilities and awareness [of, for example, magnetic tape]. Or . . . one may give up the desire to control sound, clear one's mind of music, and set about discovering means to let sounds be themselves rather than vehicles for man-made theories or expressions of human sentiment" (S10).[17] To which Cage adds, Zen-like: "It goes without saying that dissonances and noises are welcome in this new music" (S11). Nothing is to be excluded. For every sound, in and of itself, is a perfection of existence:

> A sound does not view itself as thought, as ought, as needing another sound for its elucidation, as etc.; it has no time for any consideration—it is occupied with the performance of its characteristics: before it has died away it must have made perfectly exact its frequency, its loudness, its length, its overtone structure, the precise morphology of these and of itself.
>
> Urgent, unique, uninformed about history and theory, beyond the imagination, central to a sphere without surface, its becoming is unimpeded, energetically broadcast. There is no escape from its action. It does not exist as one of a series of discrete steps, but as transmission in all directions from the field's center. It is inextricably synchronous with all other sounds, non-sounds, which latter, received by other sets than the ear, operate in the same manner.

A sound accomplishes nothing; without it life would not last out the instant. (S14)

If the modern tradition of sound poetry were to take the form of an argument, it would be an argument in behalf of these two theses, that sound entails a critique or displacement of the cognitive subject exercising rational control and that this in turn makes possible an openness and responsiveness, an acceptance of sound as such, with no more in-sounds versus out-sounds. The argument would be Levinasian in what it calls for or what it asks of us, namely, something like an ethical or prophetic attitude toward sound as voice, with even ordinary sounds somehow aspiring to the condition of the voice. And it would be Cage-like—that is, comic and demystifying—in its development, as in Cage's stated preference for cowbells over Beethoven. Noise and dissonance are no longer to suffer the logic of exclusion. Tuning out is a form of dying, whereas listening, as Cage says, "is simply a way of waking up to the very life we're living, which is so excellent once one gets one's mind and one's desires out of its way and lets it act of its own accord" (S12).

By "comic and demystifying" I mean this: Sound poetry has nothing of the monumentality and solemnity of the *Grand Œuvre*. The world of high art is deaf to it. It rarely or never makes its way into museums, performance halls, libraries, classrooms, or workshops. It is surely out of place in a great lecture hall. Inevitably it causes people to laugh. And indeed one should reflect on the internal link between sound and laughter in contrast to the link between silence and gravity: Irrepressibility is a condition of both sound poetry and laughter as against the controlled conditions of the church, the recital hall, and the schoolroom. Perhaps, one could argue, sound is inherently comic precisely because of its resistance to repression or containment, its ability to penetrate walls and to invade us like sprites. Excess defines the ontology of sound, which is perhaps why poetry exploits it. In any case, sound is a sign of life, or of things happening, whereas silence is of the grave.[18] But for Cage silence is a fiction, or a purely theoretical condition, because it is always being interrupted by sound, even when we try not to hear it. As Cage remarks in "Experimental Music," "try as we may to make a silence, we cannot" (S8). In fact, we can only simulate a silence by producing a sound and then pausing. (What is interesting is that even then there are inaudible sounds, or sounds inaudible to the human ear, or some human ears; and there are private sounds, like those produced by tinnitus.)

There are at present at least two indispensable texts for beginning a study of sound poetry. The first is by the intermedia artist and Fluxus crony Dick Higgins, "A Taxonomy of Sound Poetry," which is to be found in a collection of his pieces called *Precisely: Ten Eleven Twelve*, although the text is perhaps most accessible on UbuWeb (www.ubu.com), a Web site devoted to visual and sound poetry as well as other experimental poetic forms.[19] The second text is by the poet Steve McCaffery, a founding member of the legendary Canadian sound-poetry group the Four Horsemen. McCaffery is a sound poet in his own right, and for me he is the most innovative and conceptually challenging poet now writing. His essay "Voice in Extremis" is a fairly detailed history of sound poetry in all of its forms. The essay appears in McCaffery's *Prior to Meaning: The Protosemantic and Poetics*.[20] I take "protosemantic" to be an essentially anarchic concept in the Levinasian sense of being on the hither side of mind or spirit, namely, the sensible or fleshly side of signification, which is where the voice exists as the physical excess or remainder of what it otherwise accomplishes as a medium that expresses a meaning, a psychological interior, or a cognitive presence. Imagine the voice as a limit or resistance rather than a presence (the way a *grating* voice blocks attention to what the voice is saying). Here the concept of materiality so central to modernist poetics undergoes an important amplification: In addition to the materialist's materiality of social conditions and the modernist's materiality of language, there is also the materiality of the poet's body. Breath is an immediate example; however, imagine breath not simply (as in Charles Olson) as a line break but rather now purely and simply (or materially) as *sound*.[21]

What kind of sound? As a thought experiment, we should make a list of all the sounds that a human mouth can make. Besides vocal there are buccal sounds—"buccal" means "of or pertaining to the cheek." The mobility of sound is rooted in the rubbery flexibility of cheeks, without which the mouth is useless. Think also of lips kissing and popping and simulating farts. Don't forget glottal sounds made with the tongue (clucking, trilling) or guttural sounds made with the throat: choking, for example, or swallowing, gurgling, hawking, grunting, growling, hiccupping. Then there are bronchial sounds: breathing, gasping, wheezing, coughing. And nasal sounds: sniffing, snoring, sneezing, whinging, speaking French. Not to mention dental sounds: teeth clicking, chattering, grinding. Buccal sounds are proto- or extralingual: They break with the phonetic world that underwrites language. This is even more true when the sounds of the voice, mouth, teeth, and sinus are augmented or modified technologically. (It matters that *anyone* can make a sound poem.) A good example of the range or variety of vociferations that are humanly possible can be found in Steve McCaffery's "Mr. White in Panama."

[Play Steve McCaffery's "Mr. White in Panama"]

Dick Higgins in his essay sees the history of modern poetry in terms of a shift from a normative "art of power" toward an "art of experience" in which the poem is liberated from uses of language justified by meaning or authorized by canonical aesthetic forms; the idea, he says, is to relocate the poem within the order of events rather than within the order of objects. He cites the *zaum* poetry of the Russian futurists, F. T. Marinetti's *parole in libertà*, and Hugo Ball's *lautgedichte* as critical breaking points in which sound ceases to be a semantic, or even a prosodic, medium and becomes constitutive of the poem (or the poetic performance) itself. Of course, in these examples sound is still tied to language—or at least to the phonetic alphabet—even when the language is unknown, spoken nowhere, invented, simulated, or confounded with others. In fact, even today much of sound poetry remains text based.

Or does the text undergo a kind of mutation when its intentionality is oriented toward the experience of sound as such? Richard Kostelanetz, for example, coined the term "text-sound texts" in order to distinguish texts to be heard from those meant to be seen and read: "The term 'text-sound' characterizes a language whose principal means of coherence is sound, rather than syntax or semantics—where the sounds made by comprehensible words create their own coherence apart from

prelude:

Fümms bõ wõ tãã zãã Uu,
     pögiff,
       kwii Ee.

    1

Oooooooooooooooooooooooooooooooooo,

    6

dll rrrrr beeeee bõ,   (A) 5
dll rrrrr beeeee bõ fümms bõ,
rrrrr beeeee bõ fümms bõ wõ,
  beeeee bõ fümms bõ wõ tãã,
    bõ fümms bõ wõ tãã zãã,
      fümms bõ wõ tãã zãã Uu:

first movement:

theme 1:
Fümms bõ wõ tãã zãã Uu,
     pögiff,
       kwii Ee.

    1

theme 2:
Dedesnn nn rrrrrr,   2
      Ii Ee,
         mpiff tillff too,
            tillll,
               Jûû Kaa? (*sung*)

theme 3:
Rinnzekete bee bee nnz krr müü?   3
          ziiuu ennze, ziiuu rinnzkrrmûû,

  rakete bee bee.   3 a

theme 4:
Rrummpff tillff toooo?   4

Figure 1. "Der Ursonate," by Kurt Schwitters

transitìon:

Ziiuu ennze ziiuu nnzkrrmüü,
Ziiuu ennze ziiuu rinnzkrrmüü,

rakete bee bee? rakete bee zee.   ü 3 a

development:

Fümms bö wö tää zää Uu,
Uu zee tee wee bee fümms.

    rakete rinnzekete   **(B)**   ü3+
    rakete rinnzekete   3 a
    rakete rinnzekete
    rakete rinnzekete
    rakete rinnzekete
    rakete rinnzekete
    Beeeee
    bö.

fö   1
    böwö
fümmsbö
    böwörö
fümmsböwö
    böwörötää
fümmsböwötää
    böwörötääzää
fümmsböwötääzää
    böwörötääzääUu
fümmsböwötääzääUu
    böwörötääzääUu pö
fümmsböwötääzääUu pö
    böwörötääzääUu pögö
fümmsböwötääzääUu pögö
    böwörötääzääUu pögiff

ü 3

Phoneme Dance for/from John Cage
(A Word Event for John Cage) 9/28/74

(Pronounce each letter separately—no diphthongization—& with the following qualities: "a" as in "day"; "o" as in "hot"; "j" as in "joy"; "k" as in "kite"; "n" as in "tin". Use relative sizes of spaces to regulate durations of silence between phoneme groups. Read carefully & as slowly as comfortable; let a lot of time go by for vertical spaces.)

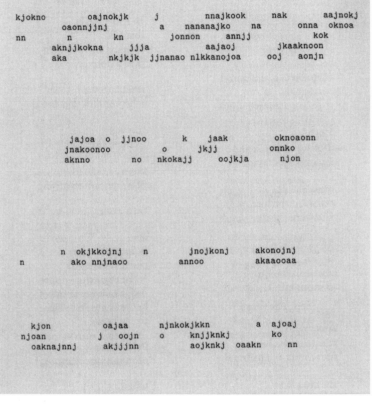

```
kjokno        oajnokjk      j          nnajkook     nak        aajnokj
              oaonnjjnj     a      nananajko    na       onna  oknoa
nn        n       kn        jonnon     annjj              kok
     aknjjkokna     jjja              aajaoj          jkaaknoon
     aka          nkjkjk  jjnanao nlkkanojoa       ooj  aonjn




              jajoa  o  jjnoo      k   jaak         oknoaonn
              jnakoonoo          o   jkjj           onnko
              aknno           no  nkokajj    oojkja     njon




        n  okjkkojnj     n       jnojkonj    akonojnj
  n        ako  nnjnaoo           annoo       akaaooaa




    kjon          oajaa      njnkokjkkn       a   ajoaj
  njoan        j    oojn     o    knjjknkj         ko
  oaknajnnj      akjjjnn          aojknkj  oaakn      nn
```

Figure 2. "Phoneme Dance for/from John Cage," by Jackson Mac Low

SOL AIR

Poème-1961. Audio-poème 1964. Pour ballet et choréographie.
Durée: 10'. Superpositions timbrales: 4. Exclusivement realize par la voix de l'auteur.
Recherche: fission de particules bucchales et timbrales, anatomie du verbe.
Composition intégrale avec les deux mots precedents: soit Sol et Air.
Vitesses du magnétophone: 9,5 cm
                          19 cm
                          4,75 cm
Mixage en studio. Recueilli sur v. 38 cm/s.

v. 9,5 cm: soooooolrrrrrrrrrrrrr
                  rrrrrrrrrrllossssssssS   SôôôLRRRRRRR
                  siiiiiiiiiiiiiiiiiii   (" s " = spirance)
                  airfffle (variation) rrrrlllooooooosssSSS so air rrrRRR
                  soooooolrrrrrrrrrrr   sssssssssssssssss....

                  fragments pour 10 " sur une piste.

v. 9,5 cm: rrrrrrrrrrrrr **(appoints claquements de lèvres)**
                  iiiiiiiiiiiiiiiiiii **(pizzicato sur v. 4, 75 cm " aigü)**

                  s

                    o

                     l

                           a i r (chute du timbre presque inaudible)
                  (recouvert par) sol RRR
                               rrrr LosSSS (recurrence)
                  fragments pour 10" sur une autre piste.

v. 4,75 cm:

                  (exclusivement des aigus soit des: claquements de lèvres et bouches, des
                  voyelles <<e>> couvrant les enregisments precedents; emploi de
                  plus du volume sonore part augmentation des intensités ou diminution.
                  Superpositions: 4)

                  l i l i lll ii l i lllll iii l iiiiiiiiii l i l i l
                  SSS OOOOOOS   (puis liquide) èèèèèè .... (dimi-
                                                            nuendo) RRRR

Figure 3. "Sol Air," by Henri Chopin

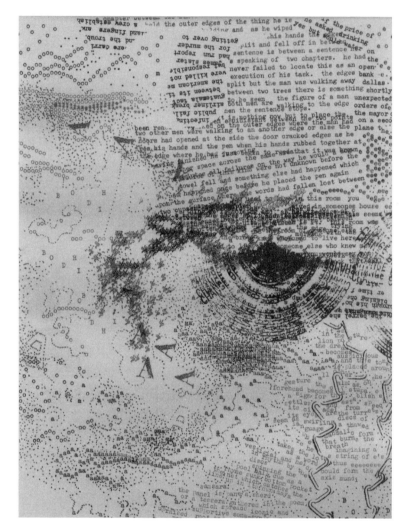

Figure 4. "Carnival 1," by Steve McCaffery

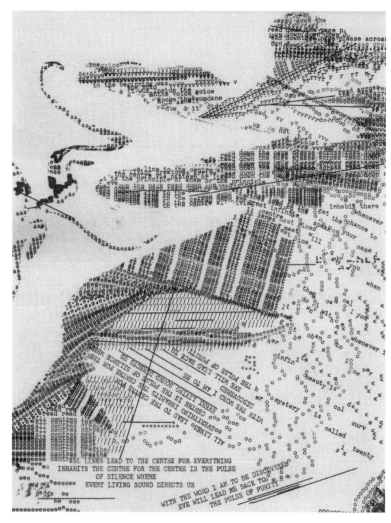

Figure 5. "Carnival 2," by Steve McCaffery

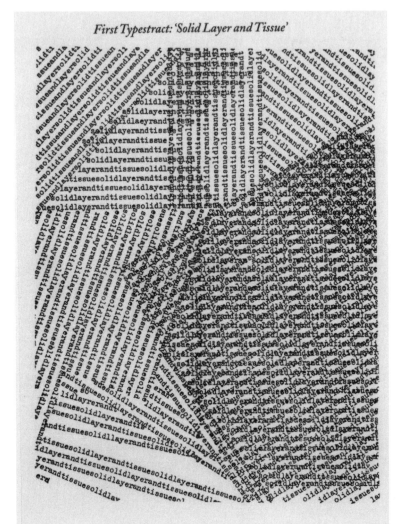

Figure 6. "First Typestract," by Steve McCaffery

Figure 7. "Bilingual Typestract," by Steve McCaffery

denotative meanings."[22] (What is even more interesting is that, when printed, the text-sound text looks like a visual or concrete poem. See the postscript to this chapter.) An early "text-sound text" is "Der Ursonate," by the dadaist or Merz artist Kurt Schwitters, which is a sonata for the speaking voice with an alphabetic score. (See figure 1.)

[Play Christian Bök's version of Kurt Schwitter's "Der Ursonate"]

The text-sound text is not something to be deciphered but something to be performed, and so poetry becomes (whatever else it may be or remain) a species of *theater*. Poetry is no longer performed as a reading but becomes itself a performance art; it is no longer an object but an event in which the distance between performer and audience breaks down completely.[23] Sound poetry aims at the construction not of works but of situations or environments that place the audience in what Allan Kaprow called a "state of immersion." Sound, after all, is more like a liquid than a solid. There is no grasping, fixing, framing, or settling it.[24] We are always *inside* of sound, which in turn fills us as we listen to it. We should see ourselves, or hear ourselves, as containers of sound.

The work of the American poet Jackson Mac Low deserves greater study in this regard. His *gathas*, "word events," and "vocabularies" are prefaced by "performance instructions" in which listening is stressed as a condition of performance, indeed as part of the poem itself. "Phoneme Dance for/from John Cage" is a good example. In this work, the letters that make up John Cage's name are the script or score: "Pronounce each letter separately—no diphthongization—& with the following quali-ties: 'a' as in 'day'; 'o' as in 'hot'; 'j' as in 'joy'; 'k' as in 'kite'; 'n' as in 'tin.' Use relative sizes of spaces to regulate durations of silence between phoneme groups. Read carefully and slowly as comfortable; let a lot of time go by for vertical spaces."[25] (See figure 2.) The instructions for "A Vocabulary for Custer LaRue," a "simultaneity" for several voices, musi-cal instruments, and the phonemes in the name "Custer LaRue," specify that "Performers must *listen* carefully to all sounds in the environment, especially other performers, but also audience & other ambient sounds, & *relate* whatever they are doing with whatever they are hearing. They must be sensitive, tactful, & courteous as well as inventive."[26]

Mac Low's "simultaneities" are an attempt to break down the hierarchy of composer/performer/audience as well as the formal structures that put the voice in the service of music and language. The idea is to construct a form of performance in which *several* voices, languages, and musical sounds occupy simultaneously the same temporal field, like one of John Cage's musicircuses, whose goal is to set in motion a number of processes or events that do not form a progression or a structure but simply happen together, come what may. One can see this happening-together as an anarchic form of community, as Steve McCaffery suggests when he refers to the sound-poetry *group* as "the manifestation of unpremeditated and ephemeral collectivity" (PM183). Such a community is *acephalic*, or headless, and it is not meant to last. This communal conception is also consistent with Cage's notion of theater:

> For a calculated
> theatrical activity I would say offhand that
> the minimum number of necessary actions going on
> at once is five. Bright people can clear up
> rather quickly perplexity arising from lower numbers (S173)

[Play Jackson Mac Low and Anne Tardos's "Phoneme Dance for/from John Cage"]

As "Phoneme Dance" suggests, Mac Low is a *phonetic* sound poet, in contrast to the French artist Henri Chopin, a nonphonetic poet or, as he prefers, an *audio-poet*. In the late 1950s and early 1960s, Chopin facilitated the work of several writers and artists whose experiments introduced a radical break between poetry and writing: François Dufrêne, Paul de Vree, and Gil Wolman, among many others. (Chopin was the editor of the journal *OU: Cinquième saison*, whose issues had sleeves containing recordings of sound poems.) Sometimes members of this group referred to themselves as *Ultralettristes* in order to distinguish themselves from Isidore Isou's group, the *Lettristes*, whose main orientation was toward visual or typographic poetry—Isou used the terms "metagraphics" or "hypergraphics" to describe the poetry, which was made of Greek and Roman alphabets, ideograms, and phonetic notations. The *Lettristes*, however, as Steve McCaffery notes, also assigned "nonphonetic values" to letters of the alphabet: O calls for coughing, P for clicking the tongue (PM171). In fact some of Isou's sound poems dating from 1947 can be heard on UbuWeb. Many of both sets of artists combined sound and letter poetry into single compositions, as in Henri Chopin's "Sol Air." (See figure 3.)

[Play Henri Chopin's "Sol Air"]

Henri Chopin, perhaps more than anyone else in this company, aimed not only at the production of inarticulate sounds but also, with the help of tape recorders, microphones, and other technological equipment, extreme acoustical experiences.

[Play Henri Chopin's "Vibrespace"]

McCaffery writes, "Subjected to Chopin's creativity, technology functions first and foremost as a heuristic, amplificatory prosthesis, supporting an exploratory poetry of interior intensities, an art that unfolds the romantic interior self, at once demythologizing human interiority (as the *hegemonikon*, the scholastic site of the soul) and debunking traditional, anatomical prohibitions" (PM178–79). So, once more, sound is critique in which the subject is materialized or reembodied in "the body's noise": "Paying attention to the body's heterological sonic phenomena [Chopin] transforms them into a powerful expressive vocabulary, manipulating tensions between the microsonic and its amplified exteriorization, making manifest an art of the insensible made sensible through the magnifying powers of the tape recorder" (PM179). Here we discover that the sounds of the body can be more violent, more intrusive, than the body's touch.

François Dufrêne's "crirhythmes" differ from Chopin's audio-poems because they retain the corporeality of sounds produced by the voice and mouth. Dufrêne's sound poetry is, to use the term Steve McCaffery applies to the Canadian sound groups of the 1970s, "paleotechnical" (PM182): a species of body art in which one experiences the voice as a force or an energy rather than as a kind of electronic acoustical instrument.

[Play François Dufrêne's "Batteries vocales"]

McCaffery quite rightly emphasizes the connection between Chopin's and Dufrêne's poetics and Georges Bataille's concept of "free expenditure" (*dépense*), in which one spends one's energy, one's wealth, one's self or life or voice, without any interest in a return on one's investment (PM178). *Dépense* implies an economy of loss or waste rather than one of accumulation; it is heterogeneous or anarchic with respect to every order based on a system of exchange, including the exchange of letters for sounds, words for meanings, and commands for obedience. It is, as McCaffery says, a "libidinal economy."[27] Inspired by Bataille, Chopin, along with Isidore Isou and the Situationist Guy Debord, anticipated Gilles Deleuze and Felix Guattari in thinking of language as essentially imperative in its function: "Language is made not to be believed but to be obeyed, and to compel obedience. . . . A rule of grammar is a power marker before it is a syntactical marker."[28] Chopin says, "The Word today serves no one except to say to the grocer: give me a pound of lentils."[29] Hence, to break with language is to break with the order of rules.

Chopin and Dufrêne are also explicitly theatricalizing the voice in ways first imagined by Antonin Artaud in the 1930s in his writings on "the theater of cruelty."[30] For Artaud, theater is like the plague in which everything is permitted, that is, in which the rules and conventions, the laws and taboos, that govern the world of the audience have been abandoned (TD24). Theater is a space of absolute negative freedom. Moreover, theater originates on the stage, not behind the scenes: The director replaces the playwright (TD60). "No more masterpieces" is Artaud's motto—no more "subjugation of the theater to the text." The space of theater is "not psychological but plastic and physical." It is a space of pure performance. The task of the voice in this event is not to *articulate* language, speech, or dialogue but rather to *materialize* itself in the form of cries, groans, strangulations, and screams: "let words be joined again to the physical motions that gave them birth, and let the discursive, logical aspect of speech disappear beneath its affective, physical side, i.e., let words be heard in their sonority rather than taken for what they mean grammatically" (TD119).[31] ("No one in Europe," Artaud complained, "knows how to scream anymore," although, of course, the Nazis were already teaching people the art [TD141].)

Theatricalizing language and voice means corporealizing them, reinserting them into the body. Artaud's theater is meant to act *on* the audience, not for it or in front of it. Theater is meant to be felt like a blow to the head or viscera. Its purpose is to attack normative states of mind formed and fixed by the constraints of a rationalized society. As Artaud says, theater works by "resisting the economic, utilitarian, and technical streamlining of the world" (TD122)—and its resistance is anything but passive. The idea is to use the voice "in a new, exceptional, and unaccustomed fashion; to reveal its possibilities for producing physical shock; to divide and distribute it actively in space; to deal with intonations in an absolutely concrete manner, restoring their power to shatter as well as really to manifest something; to turn against language and its basely utilitarian, one could say alimentary sources, against its trapped-beast origins" (TD46). A theatricalized voice is one that induces fear.

Artaud underscores the way in which philosophical, political, and aesthetic forms of anarchism provide a conceptual framework for the history of sound poetry. What this means—and whether it adds up to a *defense* of sound poetry—probably depends on how well we can cope with anarchy and anarchism as positive concepts, which in fact is what artists like John Cage, Jackson Mac Low, and, as I read or hear him, Steve McCaffery encourage us to do. One way to proceed would be to distinguish between two kinds of discourse: those that aim at truth and those whose purpose is freedom. What the first requires is the regimentation of language and the subjection of its use to rigorous truth conditions, what Michel Foucault would call "normalcy," a state "produced by multiple forms of constraint" set out by society, the chief consequence of which would be that very little would be said and possibly everything that is true could be reduced to or entailed within a single statement. What the second requires is the abandonment of principles and rules (Foucault would count sound poetry as a discourse of madness), because their main function is to exclude certain uses or practices, especially those that allow language to career out of control or to expend itself without reason or profit.[32] What is worth noticing is that these two kinds or aims of discourse are interdependent or at least not mutually exclusive; rather, the one is necessarily presupposed by the other, and vice versa. The philosopher Bernard Waldenfels characterizes this state of affairs by saying that there is neither a realm of freedom outside of all regimentation, rarefaction, and restraint nor a rule-governed system in which power always flows in obedience to the rules:

> Something unruly is to be found within what is ruled, just as the invisible or unsayable is not beyond what is seen or said but within. This unruly may be called *sens sauvage*, a sense that cannot be completely domesticated. [John] Searle's distinction between "brute facts" and "institutional facts" has to be modified. In every work of culture there remains some brutishness, which is not to be devalued as simply awaiting rationalization or fleeing from it. Rather we should take it in the sense Dubuffet intends when he speaks of *art brut*. If we should one day succeed in taming all that resists, in ruling out the unruly and in filling in all the blanks, the game would be up.[33]

Art brut is, according to Jean Dubuffet, who introduced the concept in the 1940s, the art of outsiders—the art of the *abnormal*, to use Foucault's term: those whom rational society confines or eliminates because of the way they disturb the order of things, whether by unruly or illegal conduct or, more often, by failing to resemble, whether sufficiently or efficiently, governing category descriptions.[34] *Art brut* more generally is art that fails to satisfy the conditions (whatever they might be) that make art possible. As such, *art brut* entails (as perhaps all modernist art does) a performative contradiction in the sense that, for there to be such a thing at all, a concept of what it is has to exist, with, of course, all the stipulations that define the conditions of its existence (for example, the condition of exteriority, allowing for several senses of this term). At the same time, however, the extension of the concept cannot be closed by a frontier; arguably, therefore, such a thing as sound poetry could serve as an instance of *art brut* because of its radical exteriority with respect to a poetry constituted by the articulations of language. To be sure, not all sound poetry is merely inarticulate, but what makes sound poetry not only a genre distinction but also a limit-concept is its sheer physicality, or what Steve McCaffery refers to as "the entire foundational, animalic strata of voice and presence that connect to flight, loss, becoming, heterogeneity and heterology."[35]

A culture or society committed purely and simply to discourses of truth would, on pain of self-contradiction, have to forbid or isolate the practice of sound poetry, and probably a good deal of modern and contemporary art and poetry besides, unless it extended its concept of truth to include John Cage's openness to whatever happens, in which case a concept of truth would not be necessary or recognizable, having metamorphosed into anarchism or into a concept of negative freedom in which nothing is forbidden—a concept that, I believe, has the most fruitful application in art and theater but that also is perhaps the only coherent concept of freedom we can have.[36] Freedom of this undetermined sort is what makes the practice of sound poetry, past and future, possible. It is also why so much of sound poetry remains an art of the underground.

Postscript: A Note on the Kinship of Sound and Visual Poetry

In a course on literary modernism offered at the University of Virginia (if I remember correctly) in the fall semester of 1963, Hugh Kenner improvised the thesis that the invention of the typewriter was a more important event in the history of literature than the invention of the printing press. To be sure, the printing press changed forever the way we imagine language, as both Kenner and Walter Ong were arguing in their early research.[37] In a twinkling, moveable type transposed cultural discourse from the oral-aural world of scribal culture to the spatial-visual world of the printed book, a word container unprecedented in its appetite and mobility.[38] The technology of print made possible the construction of novels, dictionaries, and encyclopedias, as a result of which a culture of fact, information, and cumulative, if not always verifiable, *truth* settled into place. Random particles began to trump chains of being, whence the rise of realism, clutter, perspectives, and the concept of history as irreversible particulars of chance.

The typewriter is certainly more modest in the scale of its transformations.[39] At first glance, it did no more than emancipate the letter from the vagaries of the human hand, thus neutralizing, objectifying, and mobilizing the alphabet. However, the typewriter also produced, for the first time, the *page* as an aesthetic space in which the letter was no longer confined to informational structures or to the geometries of the linotype. The letter now became a *segment* capable of multidimensional arrangement *at the level of individual experiment,* as in Mallarmé's *Un coup de dés.* Although, as Dick Higgins has made clear, pattern poetry has an illustrious history antedating the typewriter—medieval manuscripts spring naturally to mind—Higgins would have to acknowledge that the typewriter transformed the lettered page into something more than a flat surface. Before the typewriter we had sheets. In fact, sheets are what get inserted into typewriters. But once inserted, the sheet is no longer two dimensional. As soon as people began experimenting with the *topography* of typography, they realized that the page could be treated as much like a volume as like a surface. The typewriter gives the page *depth* to contrast with the surface of the sheet. The sheet is no longer a white space on which letters are merely planted; it is now a mobile space that possesses a indefinite background and projected foreground that make possible multiple typographic perspectives—constellations of letters of different shapes and sizes folding into one another to form abstract (or, if one chooses, not-so-abstract) structures. The typewriter enables us to experience the *page* as an installation space, a visual field that the reader is capable of entering. The page becomes a place of occupation and activity and not simply one of perception, observation, voyeurism, decipherment, or opaque visual noise. Eugen Gomringer, one of the inventors of concrete poetry, called it a "play-area."[40]

The "pages" of Steve McCaffery's *Carnival* serve as a good example of what I mean—"a multi-panel language environment, constructed largely on the typewriter and designed ultimately to put the reader, as perceptual participant, within the center of his language." (See figures 4 and 5.)[41] The question is, How are we to read (or experience) a *page?* We begin by conceiving the page as a sculptural or architectural area— that is, the page is formed by shapes of space produced by orthographic constructions that may or may not express semantic functions, although if the letters do form words that make sense, this is likely to be experienced as an aftereffect. Kenner himself was thinking of the readerly "paralysis" induced by the *look* of a page of Pound's *Cantos*, which needs to be experienced as a spatial-visual work as much as it needs to be experienced as a discursive form. Pound's page is, after all, not just a site of words but a series of active spatial interventions controlling the disposition of letters:[42]

W. L. having run into the future non-sovereign Edvardus

on a bicycle equally freshman

a. d. 1910 or about that

beauty is difficult

in the days of the Berlin to Bagdad project

    and of Tom L's photos of rock temples in Arabia Petra

but he wd/ not talk of

    LL.G. and the frogbassador, he wanted to

    talk modern art (T.L. did)

    but of second rate, not the first rate

    beauty is difficult.

He said I protested too much   he wanted to start a press

and print the greek classics. . . . periplum

    and the very *very* aged Snow created considerable

hilarity quoting the φαίνε-τ-τ-τ-τττ-αί μοι

in reply to *l'aer tremare*

beauty is difficult

But on the other hand the President of Magdalen

(rhyming dawdlin') said there were

too many words in "The Hound of Heaven"

    a moddddun opohem he had read

and there was no doubt that the dons lived well

in the kawledg

it was if I remember rightly the burn and freeze that the fresh-

men

had failed to follow

or else a mere desire to titter etc.

and it is (in parenthesis) doubtless

    easier to teach them to roar like gorillas

than to scan φαίνεταί μοι[43]

In his essay on "Projective Verse," Charles Olson said famously that the typewriter, "due to its rigidity and its space precisions, can, for a poet, indicate exactly the breath, the pauses, the suspensions even of syllables, the juxtapositions even of parts of phrases, which he intends. For the first time the poet has the stave and the bar a musician has had."[44] This certainly has application to Pound's typographic arrangements, but Pound's page is meant to be seen as well as heard (or breathed): It is a material construction as well as a score that frees musical rhythms of speech from metronomic systems. Pound's page is rooted in what Kenner calls his "ideogrammatic method," which allows for the juxtaposition of random details in the form of collages that preserve the singularity of each detail precisely because each detail is not merely a component of or a relation in an integrated system but a word, thing, or fact in itself.[45] (Mallarmé was the first to conceive of such a system: Typography replaces syntax; it holds words together by, paradoxically, setting them apart.)[46] The detail remains visible as a vital particle occupying its own piece of the page, lying within the page as an inhabitant and not just traced on it like a foreshortened line. Kenner remarks that Pound had a special way of typing: "striking the space bar not once but at least twice, and meaning by this gesture something intrinsic to his feeling of how the lines sound and how meanings are built up. And he does this whenever he types anything, the final text of a poem or the hastiest note, and did it the day he first possessed a typewriter, circa 1913, reproducing on the machine a gesture his hand always performed when it held a pen and marked with wide spaces the initial stroke of the new word. 'Dissociate . . . ,' said Remy de Gourmont, earning his homage."[47]

The word dissociated by its surrounding space from the ongoing line or from invisible deep structures no longer merely covers over whiteness; it resides in it, giving space a contour and form as words take on a density that their conventional usage ordinarily obscures. This becomes even more true when the text on the page includes multiple and heterogeneous languages, idioms, idiolects, exotic proper names, and orthographic symbols unique to the typewriter. In this respect, much of the *Cantos* is really made of episodes of sound/visual poetry:

Amsterdam 26 April

if the houses Fiseaux, Hodshon, Crommelins, van Staphorst
5 million by August
Le corps des négociants de cette ville
souhaitant joindre leurs acclamations à ceux de toute la nation
J. Nollet, Schiedam
'On m'a dit que ces Messieurs de Schiedam
donnent ce repas de cent couverts
et qu'il y aura beaucoup de personnes de Rotterdam'
Dumas

It is true I may *open* a loan for 5 million
cash is not infinite in this country
WE THEREFORE (May 11th 1780)
accept the terms you propose 4 1/4th% for remedium
Willinck
Staphorst
Fynje

the words piddling etc/ once cost me very dear
· If you wd/ open for 3 million at first
... Van Vloten and I have agreed
3000 bonds @ 1000 francs each
Willinck
etc. (LXIX)

"Sound/visual poetry" means that words, letters, numbers, and names can be seen and sounded but not treated as panes of glass, unless after patient research one is able to transform the page into a magic-looking glass that opens onto the historical world Pound is writing about. But this contextualization does not eliminate the materiality of Pound's page. The experience of its sound/look materiality is a condition that initiates critical exegesis, which in practice means filling up the remainder of the page with supplemental writing. No one reads the *Cantos* without filling it with marginalia, which, of course, is no longer confined to the margins, there being no margins to speak of. Like the medieval Bible, the *Cantos* in its material existence becomes a glossed text, a text in which one has to gloss sound and structure as well as the words in their discursive contexts. In a real sense then the *Cantos* is an unfinished, perpetually open text. One no longer reads *between* the lines but in, out, up, down, and around them.

Pound's typographical arrangements are perhaps not as dramatic as those of his European contemporaries, particularly Guillaume Apollinaire, F. T. Marinetti, and the Russian protofuturist Ilia Zdanevich (aka Iliazd), whom Johanna Drucker has brought to life in her book *The Visible Word*. What Pound has in common with these avant-garde writers, however, is a picture of the interrelation of the visual and phonic or sonic materialities of language. Drucker notes that Marinetti deliberately confused and conflated orthography and onomatopoeia in describing his typographic experiments in *Zang Tumb, Tuuum*, but even more interesting is the way that Zdanevich used nonsemantic typographic constructions to explore the phonetic structure of Russian, thus producing, in the process, transrational or *zaum* poems.[48] Meanwhile in the 1950s a group of Brazilian writers, the Noigandres poets, took up Pound's "ideogrammatic method" as a way of constructing three-dimensional or "verbivocovisual" poems—poems to be simultaneously read, voiced, and seen as architectural or sculpted forms, as in Haroldo de Campos's "Alea I—Semantic Variations":[49]

O ADMIRÁVEL o louvável o notával o adorável
o grandioso o fabuloso o fenomenal o colossal
o formidável o assombroso o miraculoso o maravilhoso
o generoso o excelso o portentoso o espaventoso
o espetacular o suntuário o feerífico o feérico
o meritíssimo o venerando o sacratíssimo o sereníssimo
o impoluto o incorrupto o intemerato o intimorato

O ADMERDÁVEL o loucrável o nojável o adourável
o ganglioso o flatuloso o fedormenal o culossádico
o fornicaldo o ascumbroso o iragulosso o matravisgoso

o degeneroso o incéstuo o pusdentoso o espasmventroso
o espertacular o supurário o feezífero o pestifério
o merdentíssimo o venalando o cacratíssimo o sifelíssimo
o empaluto o encornupto o entumurado o intumorato

NERUM
DIVOL
IVREM
LUNDO
UNDOL
MIVRE
VOLUM
NERID
MERUN
VILOD
DOMUN
VRELI
LUDON
RIMEV
MODUL
VERIN
LODUM
VRENI
IDOLV
RUENM
REVIN
DOLUM
MINDO
LUVRE
MUNDO
LIVRE[50]

program do it yourself
the reader (or operator)
may go on at pleasure
doing new semantic variations
within the given parameter

And so we have a poem made of words that can be experienced as
an objective structure and voiced as a *score*. Likewise sound poems can
be experienced visually, which is why Richard Kostelanetz's anthology
of text-sound texts doubles as an anthology of concrete poetry (or, as

Kostelanetz sometimes calls it, *audiovisual* poetry). With reference to Mary Ellen Solt's "Zigzag," a poem made of Zs arranged on the page to form zigzags, Kostelanetz writes: "Kalvert Nelson reads it on tape setting up a rhythmic pattern of Z's from which the word 'zig-zag' gradually emerges following each step in the visual design. He also employs a rise in pitch at the beginning of each section. The poem is read straight through once. Then with the help of the sound engineer, this recording is superimposed upon itself four times in the nature of a round or canon. The final performance version consists of the original straight through reading and the final canonic version in which all of the superimpositions occur."[51] But typography and sound are not always fully convertible. Steve McCaffery's visual poems for his installation *Carnival* can be performed as sound poems, but their orientation is toward what McCaffery calls *typestracts*, in which letters condense into clusters to the point of blackout. (See figures 6 and 7.) In this case the poetic experience reduces to ink.[52]

"SQUEEZE the language material: that is what can be titled concrete." This is the motto of the Swedish concrete poet and painter Öyvind Fahlström, whose philosophy of composition is as follows: "begin with the smallest elements, letters and words. Throw the letters around as in anagrams. Repeat the letters in words; lard with foreign words, gä-elva-rna [djävlarna = devils]; with foreign letters, ahaanadala-ianaga for handling, compare with pig latin and other secret languages; vowel glissandos gäaeiouuåwrna. Of course also 'lettered,' newly discovered words. Abbreviations as new word building, exactly as in everyday language, we certainly have Mimömolan [the law of least resistance]."[53] Squeeze the materials, and meaning will be the chief extract, but do not squeeze so completely as to drain the letters and words of their "verbivocovisual" reality:

					is- o. tå-			
			ring		pallen	u-		urr
		vilt	nära	jumper				aska
	skriv		ovana		ändar	yra		
ring	glöd	ovan				bollar		
	bollar				ovan	*nypa* ·		hopp

```
              i is-
              o. tape-                                    pekoral-
              hallen    eter    ovan                      finger
                                          pekoral-
ön                      bo      löst      finger
ur        åker   askar          famnar


          löst                    ovana   BO      ändar
närande          askar                    ring            yra
          ö                       åker             ringen  buren
                 pekfing-
                 rets     vakna   åskådare                 ovana
ovana     ur     slunga   slunga
bo        ringa  ur                               askar
                                          applåd-
eter             famnar                   åska             lös
          eter   buren    om                      nära⁵⁴
```

The basic unit of this constellation is the morpheme. However, Fahl-ström's idea is that we should try not to read these words or fragments of words consecutively but to respond to the whole as a piece of abstract art. Only then can we begin a process of reading that moves in multiple directions: "the strophes can be read not only from left to right and from above to below but vice versa and vertically: all the first words in every line, then all the second, the third, etc. Mirroring, diagonal reading. Change of lines, particularly of short lines. Free emphasis and free word order as in classical literature (that we don't have the same linguistic conditions is no reason not to make these experiments)."[55]

The task of reading, in other words, is to mobilize the word constellation, to set it in motion. From here it is only a short walk to the world of digital or, more exactly, holographic poetry in which the poem is kinetic in the nature of the case. In a holographic text the page is replaced by an empty three-dimensional (actually four-dimensional) space in which words float and reconfigure themselves as readers proceed through it, perhaps reading but certainly experiencing the materiality of language in a seemingly dematerialized way. The Brazilian poet Eduardo Kac, perhaps the most important figure in this new form of art, writes:

> I create what I call holographic poems, or holopoems, which are essentially holograms and computer holograms that address language both as material and as subject matter. I try to create texts which can only signify upon the active perceptual and cognitive engagement on the part of the reader or viewer. This ultimately means that each reader 'writes' his or her own texts as he or she looks at the piece. My holopoems don't rest quietly on the surface. When the viewer starts to look for words and their links, the texts will transform themselves, move in three-dimensional space, change color and meaning, coalesce and disappear. This viewer-activated choreography is as much a part of the signifying process as the transforming verbal and visual elements themselves.[56]

The space of the poem is actually four dimensional, because the reader moves temporally through the space and so alters it (and its contents) as he or she proceeds. Here is certainly a subject for further study.[57] The idea would be to connect holographic art with early twentieth-century constructivism, which tried to create new forms of space by means of collage and assemblage, with found materials being attached to surfaces of differing kinds—pages, canvases, walls. The *Merzwerke* of Kurt Schwitters would be good to study in this context, because "Merz" meant the assembly of disparate materials into a fabricated space. The achievement of holographic art is its ability to include the reader, or viewer, among these materials and to set the whole ensemble in motion.[58]

3 Poetic Materialism

The Poet's Redemption of Everyday Things

Things are already as close to words as they are to things, and
reciprocally words are already as close to things as they are to words.
—Francis Ponge

In Hebrew the word for *word* is also the word for *thing*. The roots and
stems of grammar are foresights and hindsights so entangled that
traditions and chronologies mean little if not an acceptance, a love of
certain living things seen as things.
—Louis Zukofsky

The proximity of things is poetry.
—Emmanuel Levinas

I've argued that poetry is made of words but not of what we use words to produce (propositions, descriptions, expressions, narrations). I wonder if one could, without contradicting or rejecting this thesis, also argue that poetry is made of *things*—just plain *things*—the way Marcel Duchamp's Readymade works of art are just ordinary things that anyone could buy in a store, like a bicycle wheel or a snow shovel. Of course, tradition says that things are the property of narratives, with their weakness for lists and obsession with furniture.[1] Poems for their part are said to be made of images, like Pound's perfectly rendered piece "In a Station of the Metro":

The apparition of these faces in the crowd;

Petals on a wet, black bough.[2]

This is, strictly speaking, not a poem made of things but the record of an urban perception that triggers the memory of a "natural" one. But the perceptions are, as the New Critics used to say, *concrete*. The poetic imperative of Pound's Imagism, "Direct treatment of the thing, whether subjective or objective," means no abstractions, no universals, no statements or rhetorical figures, and above all no using the word "like."[3] The stress is on *singularity*. In William Carlos Williams's famous and even canonical words:

> —Say it, no ideas but in things—
> nothing but the blank faces of houses
> and cylindrical trees
> bent, forked by preconception and accident
> split, furrowed, creased, mottled, stained
> secret—into the body of the light![4]

The task of imagination, Williams said in *Spring and All*, is not to invent possible worlds but "to free the world of fact from the impositions of 'art.' "[5]

Art means artifice, with implications of "fake." What the poet is after, Williams says, is "not realism, but reality itself."[6] For Williams, the universality of things means that they are everywhere close at hand, not that they are conceptual or universalized objects of cognition, representation, or various forms of poetizing: "What I put down of value will have this value: an escape from crude symbolism, the annihilation of strained associations, complicated ritualistic forms designed to separate the work from 'reality'—such as rhyme, as meter and not as the essential of the work, one of its words."[7] So a poetry of things will perhaps require, as Stephen Fredman has in fact argued in *Poet's Prose*, a poetry made of prose—that is, poetry without poeticalness (recall here Williams's disagreement with Wallace Stevens, for whom the task of imagination is to make the world exotic). A poetry of things calls for ordinary speech:

> Meanwhile,
> the old man who goes about
> gathering dog-lime
> walks in the gutter
> without looking up

and his tread is more majestic than
that of the Episcopal minister
approaching the pulpit
of a Sunday.[8]

Yet there still remains the question of how *things* are to be understood
in this context, because clearly there is considerable difficulty as to how
to conceive *any* relation in poetry between words and things, especially
if the assumption or intuition is (as mine is) that this relation is not
simply one of nomination, designation, predication, or description; that
is, it is not a relationship of *mediation* linking separate entities across an
ontological divide but a relationship of proximity, intimacy, and perhaps
even identity provided by a shared plane of existence. But how, short of
appealing to magic (which no doubt I once had no trouble doing), are
we to conceive this relationship?[9] It is not clear to me that we have
the conceptual resources for dealing with this question, but there are
sources we can investigate.

One is the work of the French poet Francis Ponge, whose poem *Le
parti pris des choses* (*Taking the Side of Things*) is made of things that
do not always—in fact, never—make it across the threshold of literary
attention: a wooden crate, a cigarette, an oyster, a doorknob, a piece of
bread, snails, a pebble. Ponge is a poet of the low and indifferent, the
world beneath notice. He makes it his task to redeem these mundane
things from the oblivion to which human self-centeredness consigns
them. Here, for example, is "Le cageot" ("The Crate"):

A mi-chemin de la cage au cachot la langue française a cageot, simple
caissette à claire-voie vouée au transport de ces fruits qui de la moindre suffocation font à coup sûr une maladie.

Agencé de façon qu'au terme de son usage il puisse être brisé sans effort,
il ne sert pas deux fois. Ainsi dure-t-il moins encore que les denrées fondants
ou nuageuses qu'il enferme.

A tous les coins de rues qui aboutissent aux halles, il luit alors de l'éclat sans
vanité du bois blanc. Tout neuf encore, et légèrement ahuri d'être dans une
pose maladroite à la voirie jeté sans retour, cet objet est en somme des plus

sympathetiques,—sur le sort duquel il convient toutefois de ne s'appensantire longuement.[10]

* * *

Halfway between *cage* (cage) and *cachot* (prison cell) the French language has *cageot* (crate), a simple openwork case for the transport of those fruits that invariably fall sick over the slightest suffocation.

Put together in such a way that at the end of its use it can be easily wrecked, it does not serve twice. Thus it is even less lasting than the melting or murky produce it encloses.

On all street corners leading to the market, it shines with the modest gleam of whitewood. Still brand new, and somewhat taken aback at being tossed on the trash pile in an awkward pose with no hope of return, this is a most likeable object all considered—on whose fate it is perhaps wiser not to dwell.[11]

"The relationship between man and object," Ponge writes, "is not at all limited to possession and use. . . . Objects are outside the soul, to be sure; and yet, they are also leadweight [*plomb*] in our heads. The relationship is thus in the accusative."[12] Notice "accusative," not nominative— not a relationship of naming but one of being summoned, as if the poet were someone who is porous with respect to things, suffering or enjoying them but also, in some way, addressed or obsessed (in the etymological sense of being besieged) by them. Accordingly things are not, as in philosophy, just objects of consciousness or of acts of cognition that aim to lay bare the essence of things. Essences are transparent; they are ghostly, otherworldly concepts. Ponge's things have weight and thickness; they pressure us. "Le cageot" is about the singularity, materiality, and even perishability of what is near at hand in his environment—the crate and its cargo share the same here-and-now temporality, the same finitude or fate: There are crates and there are crates, and even no doubt a Platonic form of a crate, but *Ponge's* crate has its own peculiar identity that warrants a proper name.

"Le cageot" begins by situating its subject (its *res* or thing) in an etymological context that turns things (cages, crates, cells) into puns. For Ponge such a context is the mode of existence that words and things have in common. In this context, words are as *material* as the things they name. "[A]ll words," he says, "should be written to allow [them] their complete semantic thickness": "If one has that sensitivity to the thickness of words, to the fact that they do have a history, that they have provoked associations of different ideas in each language and in each of the periods of the evolution of language, then this provides a much thicker material, graver, much graver in the sense of weight, a material that is not superficial, which is a thing that one can mold precisely because it has the quality, the thickness, of potter's clay. It is a physical object with many dimensions."[13] So words are not the ideal objects they are said to be in logic, linguistics, and philosophy of language; they are things made of sounds, letters, and diacritical marks but also of bits and pieces of other words, morphemes, phonemes, and homophones that are embedded historically in heterogeneous contexts of usage. The boundaries that separate words from one another (and, indeed, from things) are not logical or even determinate, so perhaps we should not think of meanings as ideal objects, either. As Ponge says, meanings are weights that time attaches to a word, which is irreducible to a concept or any sort of mental entity. Forget the distinction between letter and spirit. Only at the level of their materiality do words connect with things. This seems counterintuitive, but it is the first principle of Ponge's materialist poetics: "O resources infinies de l'épaisseur de choses, *rendues* par le resources infinies de l'épaisseur sémantique de mots!" ("O infinite resources of the thickness of things, brought out by the infinite resources of the semantical thickness of words.")[14]

Thus, for example, Ponge's poem "Le pré" ("The Meadow") is not just about a particular meadow near the Lignon River at Chantegrenouille, France; it is also about the extended semantic field that the word "pré" inhabits or projects:

Ici tourne déjà la moulin à priéres,
Sans la moindre idée de prosternation, d'ailleurs,
Car elle serait contraire aux verticalités de l'endroit.

Crase de paratus, selon les etymologists Latins,
Près de la roche et du ru
Prêt à faucher ou à paître,

Préparé pour nous par la nature
Pré, pare, pré, près, prêt,

Le pré gisant ici come le participe passé par excellence
S'y révère aussi bien comme notre préfixe des préfixes,
Préfixe déjà dans préfixe, présent déjà dans present.
Pas moyen de sortir de nos onomatopées originelles.
Il faut donc y rentrer.[15]

* * *

Here the prayer box has already begun to chatter,   [*prières*]
Without in any way intending to kneel,
Because that would be contrary to the verticalities of the place.
Crasis of *paratus*, according to Latin etymologists,   [*Krasis:* contraction]
Near rock and water,   [*Près*]
Ready to be cut or eaten   [*Prêt*]
Prepared for us by nature,   [*Préparé*]
Meadow, adorned, meadow, near, ready,   [*Pré, pare, pré, près, prêt*]
The meadow lying here like the preeminent past participle
Reveres itself also as our prefix of prefixes,
Prefix already in prefix, present already in present.
No way of avoiding our initial onomatopoeias.
Therefore, let us accept them.[16]

"Le pré" is an exploration of the "semantic thickness" of a word that is at the same time an etymological field of words that includes idiomatic expressions like "sur le pré," a dueling term meaning both "on the field" and "moment of decision."[17] The point to grasp is the way etymology multiplies the relations among words and things. Ponge's punning method of composition draws heterogeneous things together into a kind of hypertext, a nonlinear or collage construction in which words and things are homophonically nested in one another like so many places or topics. Things are decontextualized and recontextualized as predicates or relatives of the meadow, which is near (*près*) a moraine and a river and also ready (*prêt*) for mowing; meanwhile the meadow in turn is internal to the prefix as its prefix and so is a kind of hyperprefix, the prefix of prefixes, prefaces, preparations, predicates, precepts, and even prayers, prairies, and parsley (*prêle*).

Ponge's poems form a sort of paratactic cosmogony, a reconstitution of the world of things on the model of an etymological dictionary, Emile Littré's *Dictionnaire de la langue française*—"You can make fun of Littré," says Ponge, "but you must use his dictionary."[18] Etymology for Ponge is a form of life, a way of experiencing the intimacy of words and things that conceptual determination—subsuming things into logical, predicatory categories—destroys. This refusal of subsumptive thinking brings the world close to hand, makes it not only visible but also palpable, neither beautiful nor sublime but corporeal. As a result, we experience it as an essentially comic world, the more so because the things that make up Ponge's cosmos are not large and grand but plain, frequently small, usually disposable, and always indifferent to human valuation, which the poet nevertheless does not hesitate, satirically, to supply, as in "Les plaisirs de la port" ("The Pleasures of the Door"):

> Le rois ne touchent pas aux portes.
>
> Ils ne connaissent pas ce bonheur: pousser devant soi avec douceur ou rudesse l'un de ces grands panneaux familiers, se retourner vers lui pour le remettre en place,—tenir dans ses bras une porte.
>
> . . . Le bonheur d'empoigner au ventre par son noeud de porcelaine l'un de ces hauts obstacles d'une pièce; ce corps à corps rapide par lequel un instant la marche retenue, l'oeil s'ouvre et le corps tout entier s'accommode à son nouvel appartement.
>
> D'une main amicable il la retient encore, avant de la repousser décidément et s'enclore,—ce dont le déclic du ressort puissance mais bien huilé agréablement l'assure.[19]
>
> *   *   *
>
> Kings never touch doors.
>
> They're not familiar with this happiness: to push, gently or roughly before you one of these great, friendly panels, to turn towards it to put it back in place—to hold a door in your arms.
>
> The happiness of seizing one of these tall barriers to a room by the porcelain knob of its belly; this quick hand-to-hand, during which your progress slows

for a moment, your eye opens up and your whole body adapts to its new apartment.

With a friendly hand you hold on a bit longer, before firmly pushing it back and shutting yourself in—of which you are agreeably assured by the click of the powerful, well-oiled latch.[20]

Here, in the same comic spirit, is a passage from "Escargots" ("Snails"):

La colère des escargots est-elle perceptible? Y en a-t-il des exemples? Comme elle est sans aucun geste, sans doute se manifeste-t-elle seulement par une sécrétion de bave plus floculente et plus rapide. Cette bave d'orgueil. L'on voit ici que l'expression leur colère est la même que celle de leur orgueil. Ainsi se rassurent-ils et en imposent-ils au monde d'une facon plus riche, argentée.

L'expression de leur colère, comme de leur orgueil, deviant brillante en séchant. Mais aussi elle constitute leur trace et les désigne au ravisseur (au prédateur). De plus elle est éphémère et ne dure que jusqu'à la prochaine puie.

Ainsi en est-il de tous ceux qui s'expriment d'une facon entièrement sub-jective sans repentir, et par traces seulement, sans souci de construire et de former leur expression comme une demeure solide, à plusieurs dimensions. Plus durable qu'eux-mêmes.

Mais sans doutee eux, n'éprouvent-ils pas ce besoin. Ce sont plutôt des héros, c'est-à-dire des être dont l'existence même est œuvre d'art,—que des artistes, c'est-à-dire des fabricants d'œuvres d'art.

Mais c'est ici que je touche à l'un des points principaux de leur leçon, qui d'ailleurs ne leur est pas particulière mais qu'ils possèdent en commun avec tous les êtres à coquilles: cet coquille, parte leur être, est en même temps œuvre d'art, monument. Elle, demeure plus longtemps qu'eux.[21]

* * *

The anger of snails: is it perceptible? Are there instances of it? Bereft of gesture, it's expressed solely, one supposes, by a more flocculent and rapid secretion of saliva. That proud drool. We see here that the expression of their anger is the same as the expression of their pride. This reassures them and they make their mark on the world in a richer, more silvery way.

The expression of their anger, as of their pride, becomes brilliant when it dries. But it also leaves a track easily spotted by ravagers (predators). Besides, it's ephemeral and lasts only until the next rain.

And so it is with all who express themselves in this way, in a purely subjective mode, without second thoughts, without bothering to construct and shape their expression into a solid dwelling of more than one dimension. More durable than themselves.

But they probably feel no such need. They are heroes, which is to say beings whose existence is in itself a work of art, rather than artists, which is to say fabricators [in the sense of forgery] of art works.

I come here to one of the main points of their lesson, which isn't peculiar to snails but is something they share with all those who live in shells: that shell, an intrinsic part of their being, is also a work of art, a monument. It endures longer than they do.[22]

"Taking the side of things" means siding with things against human egocentrism, meaning (among other things) not just anthropocentrism but human self-importance, what we might call high-culture humanism that regards "Expressions of the Spirit" as foundational, world-making, and the source of the true, good, and beautiful. Ponge, as said, is poet of the low. "I write as I write," Ponge says, "and I do not want it to be poetry. . . . I have protested at length against my classification among poets, because lyricism in general disturbs me. That is, it seems to me that there is something too subjective, a display of subjectivity which appears to me to be unpleasant, immodest. . . . That is the reason why I have chosen things, objects, so that I would always have a brake on my subjectivity, calling back the object as it exists when I write about it."[23]

In other words, Ponge calls for an antiromantic, antisubjectivist poetry: an *Objectivism.*

Just so, it is possible to read "Escargots" as an essay in poetics, one that treats the snail first as a burlesque of subjectivism but then as a model of the perfect poem: The snail is surely the lyricist par excellence, expressing its anger or pride, but Ponge then situates the snail in a process of self-creation that results in a perfectly sculpted shell. In the end the thing and the poem are one and the same, a seamless union of art and reality that the fabrications of merely human poets can only approximate. The result is not self-expression but an objective work of art—that is, a work of art that shares the ontology of the thing.

As a poet in the French tradition inaugurated by Charles Baudelaire and Stéphane Mallarmé (or at least in a certain traditional way of conceiving this tradition), Ponge is certainly an anomaly. One need only recall Mallarmé's famous line: "to create is to conceive an object in its fleeting moment, in its absence"—as if an object were a note of music. "Destruction," Mallarmé said, "was my Beatrice." If, as the joke goes, Wallace Stevens is the greatest French poet writing in English, Ponge is perhaps the greatest American poet writing in French, precisely because his poetry is rooted so mundanely in the material intimacy of words and things. Yet this intimacy still needs explaining if it is not to be merely metaphorical. We need some examples beyond those wellworn citations from Pound and Williams that I offered at the outset. What follows are three, in decreasing order of obviousness: the work of the Objectivists—and particularly of Louis Zukofsky—and the works of Gertrude Stein and Gerald Burns.

The Objectivist tradition in American poetry, which only in the last few years has received any important critical attention, is perhaps the most obvious place to look.[24] The poet Louis Zukofsky coined the term "Objectivist" in the early 1930s to identify a group of American poets, principally Charles Reznikoff, whose work, according to Zukofsky, is characterized by "sincerity" and "objectification."[25] "Sincerity" in Zukofsky's usage does not mean speaking from the heart; it means (counterintuitively, perhaps) careful attention to the things of the world and a kind of selflessness and straightforwardness with respect to them—for example, not turning them into metaphors or stand-ins for one's own experiences. "In sincerity," Zukofsky says, "shapes appear concomitants of word combinations, precursors of . . . completed sound or structure, melody or form. Writing occurs which is the detail, not mirage, of seeing, of thinking with the things as they exist, and of directing them along a line of melody" (P12). And again: "This may seem pigheaded, but the interests of poets are in particulars. Poems are only acts upon particulars" (P215). We need to develop a more precise idea of what sorts of acts Zukofsky is thinking of and what these acts do to the things themselves. Some of Zukofsky's own poems will guide us.

"Objectification" meanwhile means "the appearance of an art form as an object" (P194). "The objectivist," Zukofsky says, "is [someone who] is interested in living with things as they exist, and as a 'wordsman' he is a craftsman who puts words together into an object" (P232). Objectification defines the poetic process as an act of construction rather than one of expression.[26] Objectification means that the poem is to be understood not as a vehicle for something antecedent to it but as a thing in its own right, "an order of words that exists as another created thing in the world" (P20): Its mode of existence is objective, not subjective, in the sense that it is not reflective of the poet's self or experience but rather, as in Ponge's poetics, takes its place side by side with the things that it employs for its material. One has to imagine a poem that seeks proximity with things and not a cognitive transcendence that grasps or contains them or makes them transparent to view. (Proximity here means what the French philosopher Emmanuel Levinas means when he says: "The visible caresses the eye. One sees and hears like one touches. . . . The proximity of things is poetry.")[27]

One might say that an Objectivist, therefore, has three distinctive features. The first is perhaps already fully articulated in Keats's notion of "negative capability": The poet has no character, and even if he or she did, this would not be the subject of the poem. The poet is objective in the way the scientist is, even though of course, in the absence of method or rule, he or she is limited by perspective, as when one engages a thing in its singularity and not as an object as such (a token of a type, a species of a genus). Objectivism is, in its way, a poetics of finitude. The second characteristic of an Objectivist is that the work of such a poet is one of *materialization*, like the making of a sculpture: The words of such a poem are not a looking glass; they do not give us a transparent view of things. Their relation to things cannot be comprehended in ocularcentric terms of seeing or rendering: The Objectivist poet is not a cognitive subject vis-à-vis an objectified entity. But of course it is precisely this break with our traditional philosophical way of conceiving our relation with things—namely objectification through the formation of concepts, categories, and distinctions—that poses the problem of poetics that I'm trying to formulate. Hence, the third feature of the Objectivist: The poet is to words and things as nature is. Nature does not describe things or refer to them; it provides for their existence—and poems are among their number. In "Found Objects (1962–1926)," looking back on more than thirty years of poetic work, Zukofsky wrote:

> With the years the personal prescriptions for one's work recede, thankfully, before an interest that *nature as creator* had more of a hand in it than one was aware. The work then owns perhaps something of the look of *found objects* in late exhibits—which arrange themselves as it were, one object near another—roots that have become sculpture, wood that appears talisman, and so on: charms, amulets maybe, but never really such things since the struggles so to speak that made them do not seem to have been human trials and evils—they appear entirely *natural*. Their chronology is of interest only to those who analyse carbon fractions, etc., who love historicity—and since they too, considering *nature as creator*, are no doubt right in their curiosity. (P168)

The poem as "found object" cannot be traced back to an originating intention. It appears to have come into the world the way anything has (a stone, a plant, or, for all of that, a word: All words are found objects). A poem as a found object is one whose genesis is unknown. It is as if it had come into being on its own, which is to say naturally.

So what does an Objectivist poem look like? With Ponge still in mind as a background or guide, I want to quote a poem from Zukofsky's last volume, *80 Flowers*. On his seventieth birthday Zukofsky decided to write eighty flower-poems over the next decade, a project to be completed on his eightieth birthday. I call them flower-poems rather than poems about flowers because these poems ignore the logic of "aboutness": Like Ponge's thing-poems, they are not descriptive in the usual sense of "description," by which we usually mean narrative description or empirical word-painting that tries to give us a form of perceptual or sensory experience (recall Pound's Imagism). Here, for example, is "Lavender Cotton":

Dwarfcypress silva evergreen spineranks branchlets
downinterlace divided leaves Great Men
sainted *rare* goldyellow globes rayless
daisies allying baskingmoth summers fragrantwool
swallows return poppyleaf grayblue white
sightwort greater-celandine to pilewort porwigle
littlefig frog buttercup arid June
rare fallen gardens *lavender cotton* [28]

Supposing this to be a good example of an Objectivist poem, one would
have to conclude that such a poem is one that pretty much does without
verbs: It is a poem of substantives and the adjectives that color, shape, or
otherwise specify them. This means that the poem, however else it may
work, cannot be any sort of predication or assertion, a fact that excludes
the possibility of metaphor, simile, and other forms of substitutive arrangements, including subsumptive reasoning. Of course, it stands to
reason that an Objectivist poem would be made of nouns, but then there
is surely a question as to whether nouns deprived of verbs can still really
work as nouns. So we still need to try to find the logic of a flower-poem:
How does it work?

The idiom of the poem is not that of human speech but rather of
an entry in an herbal dictionary or encyclopedia. [29] For example, L. H.
and E. Z. Bailey's *Hortus Second: A Concise Dictionary of Gardening,
General Horticulture and Cultivated Plants in North America* contains
this entry under LAVÁNDULA (lavender):

> "**officinàlis** (*L.Spica. L. vera*). Subshrub to 3 ft.: lvs. Linear to lanceolate, to
> 2 in. long, entire, the margins revolute, white-tomentose when young: fls.
> Lavender, to ½ in. long, with ovate-pointed bracts at the whorls.

Notice the economy: Words are not to stand in the way of things, and
this means losing the verbs. But paradoxically the thing is a kind of
magnet for words. "Dwarfcypress," for example, is another name for
lavender cotton, which is a perennial (hence "evergreen") with small
spiky or spiny silver branches (hence "branchlets"). One could gloss the
poem by consulting a series of reference books, although, as Michelle

Leggott has made clear in her indispensable book *Reading Zukofsky's 80 Flowers*, one also needs to learn a good deal about the genesis of the poems by consulting, as she did, Zukofsky's notebooks. (The method of genetic criticism seems appropriate for a flower-poem.) When Louis and Celia Zukofsky moved from Manhattan to Long Island after Louis's retirement, they became avid gardeners, and reportedly a flower, plant, or shrub did not exist that they could not recognize by name. They planted a shrub of lavender cotton in their garden on March 21, 1975— J. S. Bach's birthday, which is near the feast day of Saint Joseph (March 19), when the return of swallows to San Juan Capistrano is celebrated (hence, "swallows return"). In "arid June" lavender cotton sprouts lush "goldyellow" petals. The poem mentions other flowers planted during this time: daisies, greater celandine, buttercup, pilewort. Lavender cotton is an aromatic used in storing winter clothes during the summer to protect them from moths (hence, "allying baskingmoth summers fragrantwool"). And so on.

The poem is rooted in what Heidegger called "facticity": the flower not as poetic figure but as a thing in itself, one of the "things themselves" that the phenomenological tradition in European philosophy tried to return to as an alternative to the powerhouse tradition of German idealism presided over by Hegel, for whom things in their singularity were to be annihilated and replaced by universal concepts.

But "facticity," if indeed the word has application in Zukofsky's case (or even in Ponge's), is not the *whole* story, only the easiest one. When it comes to the relation of words and things in modern poetry, the problem of problems is still to be confronted in the work of Gertrude Stein. In my first chapter I cited Stein's *Tender Buttons* as a canonical piece of paratactic writing, but it is also canonical in its radical reconceptualization of the relation between words and things:

A *Long Dress*

What is the current that makes machinery, that makes it crackle, what is the current that presents a long line and a necessary waist. What is this current.

What is the wind, what is it.

Where is the serene length, it is there and a dark place is not a dark place, only a white and red are black, only a yellow and green are blue, a pink is scarlet, a bow is every color. A line distinguishes it. A line just distinguishes it.

Tender Buttons is a poem or collection of poems in prose concerning things close at hand in Gertrude Stein's everyday life: objects, food, rooms. However, as in Ponge's case, her relation to these things is not one of knowing and thus not nominative, predicative, or descriptive. Of course, neither is it a relation of *not* knowing, but what Stein has to say about words and things suggests something deeper and more complex. In her essay "Poetry and Grammar" she writes:

> People if you like to believe it can be made by their names. Call anybody Paul and they get to be a Paul call anybody Alice and they get to be an Alice perhaps yes perhaps no, there is something in that, but generally speaking, things once they are named the name does not go on doing anything to them and so why write in nouns. Nouns are the name of anything and just naming names is alright when you want to call a roll but is it good for anything else. To be sure in many places in Europe as in America they do like to call rolls.
>
> As I say a noun is a name of a thing, and therefore slowly if you feel what is inside that thing you do not call it by the name by which it is known. Everybody knows that by the way they do when they are in love and a writer should always have that intensity of emotion about whatever is the object about which he writes. And therefore and I say it again more and more one does not use nouns.[30]

Gertrude Stein's idea is that, if you simply call things by their name, you will never get beyond mere resemblances, because a given name is the common property of many of the same things, and even proper names are not sufficiently particular, especially if one is named after an ancestor.

In any case, in *Tender Buttons* Stein is not interested in producing resemblances of things but in the things themselves, those very things with which she is on intimate terms in her everyday world—singular things that conventions of description would cover up or displace. In "Portraits and Repetition," apropos of *Tender Buttons*, Stein has this paradoxical thing to say:

[When writing *Tender Buttons*] I became more and more excited about how words which were the words that made whatever I looked at look like itself were not the words that had in them any quality of description. This excited me very much at the time.

And the thing that excited me so very much at that time and still does is that the words that make what I looked at be itself were always words that to me very exactly related themselves to that thing the thing at which I was looking, but as often as not had as I say had as I say nothing whatever to do with what any words would do that described that thing.[31]

How can words make what we look at *be itself,* that is, not its likeness but just itself? Imagine words that *belong* with things, belong in their company, in their proximity, but that neither name nor describe them. Possibly words that name or describe things have to preside over them in some way. The "Long Dress" in the poem of that name is not described; it is presented—presented, moreover, not as something worn but as something made (of "line and . . . waist") on a sewing machine or presented as something in a certain way by the wind or by its "serene length" folded into its colors. "A line distinguishes it." So what we get is the life of the thing, how it is in the environment it inhabits. In this respect it is like one of Heidegger's things in the world around us and that we experience not as predicates or as entities as such but *circumspectly* as things at hand. Exotic things, museum pieces, clues, and valuables are objects to be inspected. But circumspection (*Umsicht*) is a term of habitation, not one of inspection or observation.[32] In our life with things, we do not keep them under surveillance. Circumspection captures exactly both Gertrude Stein's relation with the things around her *and* her poetics, the circumspect way her words make things be themselves.

Of course, it is traditional to read *Tender Buttons* as a species of abstract art—a cubist collage of words, for example, where the "Long Dress" is more like Duchamp's nude than like one of his Readymades. As Bill Brown says in *A Sense of Things: The Object Matter of American Literature,* in Stein "an apparent recognition of the physical object world . . . transforms into linguistic experiment."[33] But perhaps for Brown to say this is to reduce things too much to what can be visualized (things in novels rather than poetic things); it forestalls the Emersonian idea that a thing removed (that is, abstracted) from its environment—picked up and held for observation—ceases to be what it is, as if its identity were not logically or essentially internal to itself but were worldly and contextual, embedded (as William James or, for that matter, Heidegger would have said) in the temporality of existence. To lift it out of its temporality is to objectify it, place it on exhibit. The poems in *Tender Buttons* are not exhibits (although, to be sure, Gertrude Stein did call them "portraits").

Possibly, we are losing the thread of what a thing is, but the moral of Stein's story, as well as Ponge's and Zukofsky's, is that there is no such thing as a *generic* thing, a *Ding an sich*, but only singularities that exist beneath the reach of concepts and categories. What counts as a thing differs from Ponge to Zukofsky and from Zukofsky to Stein—recall how the one removes the verbs and the other the nouns from the realm of poetic diction. But all three play havoc with our notions of referentiality, a term whose application obstructs our relations with things, as was Heidegger's argument in section 35 of *Being and Time*, with its critique of assertion as a derivative mode of understanding things.

Let me conclude with a final example of thing-poetry. Gerald Burns, who died a short time ago, is a poet, as well as a painter and magician, who has not received much press from commentators on contemporary poetry, but his work seems to me remarkably close in form and spirit to that of Francis Ponge. Burns is a language poet who is, as I noted earlier, critical of the paratactic, protosemantic style that I praised in my first two chapters. As an alternative, he writes poems in what one might call a prose of extension. The following is from a poem entitled "The Perfect World [first approximation]":

One goes to a yard sale not to buy things but to see tired objects in a stressed relation. Hope makes you want to see things lost like condensation on the fiesta pitcher full of Koolaid; words stay ordinary as cameras without their cheap plastic cases, the cheapening effect of naming objects. Nothing is a list. The patient on the operating table, as Eliot

observes,

is an arrangement, and objects are our kindly feelings toward them. So

"objects" is itself a joke, delicious pretense of objectivity in some cool Beuys
room dedicated by the word (or hung chalkboards standing for theory) to
exhibition. The point is that any theory will do. The pig is the granular
surface of the football, also the word is. A show in D-Art in Dallas included
Greg Metz's pig's head in a coffin, and as O'Hara's
        loved
days go by went by it smelt like a funeral parlor with failed air conditioning,
the structure of the pig so useful for dissection also like it at the level of
    bacterium effluvium.
                                        Rauschenberg's painting
of a Civil War coffin would not be improved particularly with a touch of this
    smell,
but you can see how the carcase might wish to define itself, Chamberlain
    mortuary of
        wonderful car colors
underwritten by chrome. There's a way of being at home with things. One
very nice blond gent sat barefoot in shorts in shadow from a square canopy
he'd raised on poles, the blue plastic with waffle grid like no blue in nature
    now a tarp
playing a harmonica. I grabbed an easel and painted him in front of his
    boring house.[34]

What ties Ponge, Zukofsky, Stein, and Burns together is this intimate,
nonobjectifying spirit in which they bring words to bear on things that
are ordinary, everyday, beneath notice, disposable, and therefore price-
less and honorable for their subversion of official schemes of value. Burns
says, "There is a way of being at home with things." Things are, in the
end, not possessions but companions. Imagine going to a yard sale not
to buy something but to pay a visit for which, alas, we lack a theory—a
theory of browsing, perhaps. In "A Thing about Language for Bernstein,"
Burns writes: "Max Picard says if words didn't go out of themselves or
refresh themselves *in* things, they would hang around in heaps and im-
pede our movements, like things in a warehouse. That *may* be an argument for reference. One could prefer the warehouse, as one dreams
in a surplus-parts store. Will this be sought out or printed—ever be
more than *browsing*. And is there, built into some kinds of experiment, a

result, the utility of browsing only" (TL2). In an essay on contexts Burns speaks of "pottering about" (TL53) as a way of inhabiting one's own plain space, although, of course, the space is not one's own but a kind of socialist space that no one owns but which everyone and everything inhabits.

Nor is the space so plain because, as Burns says, "The world is almost intrinsically flotsam."[35] Accordingly, as a way of fitting into the world, Burns writes poems made of clutter. His shorter poems read like random inventories of things lying around, often uselessly—he calls them "prose objects" to distinguish them from exquisite things that Walter Pater or Wallace Stevens might have turned into objects of aesthetic experience. But for Burns nonaesthetic things—not only old, frequently broken things that accumulate in garages but also trivial remembered things—*are* exquisite. In "The Prose Object," a sort of poem-essay in prose, Burns writes, "Perhaps the objects we have when small are real, a pressed-steel black telephone with metal dial that we once painted white so badly, or large cardboard cartons stuck with gas station trash bulbs to be machines" (TL72). "That objects have needs is probable," Burns says (TL72). "Wristwatch straps or knobs off pots aren't meant to be unattended, or have a limit in use" (TL74). In part, Burns's text is a brief in defense of provincialism, being at home in the middle of everyday debris instead of dreamily inhabiting a quest-romance: "Provinciality, the being in a province, will depend on playing with things, whipstock sockets or other, including clumsiness like trying to hammer with a screwdriver handle" (TL73).

As it proceeds, however, "The Prose Object" metamorphoses into a collage of ordinary things assembled surrealistically from incongruous contexts—"Things unwrapped from camels would include treasures, like my kitchen shears" (TL76):

Spoerri did a topographical map of his worktable and issued a catalog, like Victoria's, of descriptions—the tiny pocketable items which since Stein and Picasso are *trendlich.* Enormous queen (but short) to be in silver-gilt on her own table, with the compotes with dogs and dead rats. What went wrong, this particularity of mixed materials, as Georgian verse didn't number the cattails or the river. There are marsh imaginings; what is a silver thistle letter opener? In the street everywhere with disposable beverage closers are red plastic moulded tail lights, each different, and lately brass key for a lock like my new bicycle's that didn't fit, bars of an electric heater seen in a trash barrel Monday, after a visit to the gallery with African masks, royal carved throne-stools, crescent wood boxes and carved bowls—perspiration dried on everything. No seeds caught in a headdress, images of the wearer (except beautifully stylized)— take us, little red plastic brakelight, you have been rendered by Mahaffey as (in the middle) a whitehot yellow, but that was in Manhattan. (TL78)

(One can't help noticing that this critic of paratactic writing was in fact a master of the form.) The reference to Spoerri is helpful. Daniel Spoerri is a Romanian artist whose signature pieces are paintings or assemblages of found objects. These objects sometimes belong together, as in his paintings of dinner tables after dinner, with cigarette butts, half-empty wine glasses, a soiled tablecloth, plates and silverware showing the remains of food, and so on. Other assemblages (in the tradition of the *Wunderkammer*, the cabinet of curiosities) gather together incongruous things—*Topographie des Zufalls*, Spoerri sometimes calls them: topographies of coincidences. Burns's *Shorter Poems* are topographies of this sort. For example, his "Another Pebble," a sort of homage to Ponge, is about fractures in stones (and things):

                    like the heavy round
ones we saw like crystallized gunpowder in the
New Age shop that're supposed to go to nothing,
discreate, if struck wrong or something, the
median line strong, as on the quite large
hailstones that falling once at SMU, catchable out
Dallas Hall's georgian windows this sometimes wavy
seam (like a sea-cucumber's side stripe) had me
thinking about faults, the Fall, Lucretius, just
from holding this translucent chunk that if candy'd
taste of wintergreen, well Michael these rocks of
yours in garden beds are that for me, incipiently
split. Ponge's *Pebble* comes from cliff face, more of
these in MacDiarmid's *Stony Limits*, as if anything not

Da Rock itself has in it shear, acknowledgment of
parametric frangibility. . . . My own variant, probably
still in Sommerville asphalt, on the Figure of Outward's a
soda can near the bus depot so much a monstrance for all
happened-on virtue even its photo . . . And you, knowing
the tone, will believe without proof, the grumble of gravel
if not in any bag you carry then all over your private desk
and alcove surfaces, found stones obscuring white paint, mahogany,
habit like a child's of bringing outdoor things inside, that
maybe moves us to pick up washers or slugs, bolts in U shapes,
hollow metal half balls recessed in squares, run-over necklace
chains and hook earrings, square nails, used car fuses so like
phials, the perfect moulded taillight ruby plastic shells, too
common silver paperclips, often large, wires with flat connectors,
coins, never foreign, though I did once find a Dallas Transit
Token under matting, these flakings off, as if of incandescent
metal from giant steel rhombi, or Brunetto's skin in Dante, off
monolith company factories on their sides huddling crystalline
out of the ground, not unwanted, not tristely discarded like an
infant or cast-iron inkstand for which you've now something
Napoleonic, and not like less-needed words, *buhl, marchpane,*
not even like (say) rhetoric imagined as the giant calipers and
magnetic cranes to push around scrap steel, cubed cars, otherwise
valuable—no, not these, even, not anything hidden in the
assumption *struktur,* but more like Aristotle's wise remark that
anything which can fall apart will, that *if* the substance you're
fond of has in it anything, not necessarily "fracture," it will
fracture, the shear plane no matter how surprising already
indicated (as, say, snake's poison) by a kind of belt or maybe
just orientation suggesting middle, something for grasping hands,
avoiding, to posit as where it will open or unscrew, some urban
notion that not everything needs bashing.[36]

"Another Pebble" is a kind of *De rerum natura* whose thesis is that it is in
the nature of things to splinter into pieces of refuse, because everything

particular is made of particles that stick together for only so long before dispersing randomly across the local land- or streetscape. Look closely and you'll see that everything is seamed ("incipiently split"). Nevertheless these things lost or ruined return to make a claim on the poet (as on children) to treat them as treasures—or as "found objects," a species of things that doubles as a genre of art.[37]

This doubling of found things as art things defines, of course, the work of Joseph Cornell, whose constructions are boxes filled with ordinary objects and images of familiar things, each of which resonates with a peculiar surrealist density because of the strange way it has been recontextualized.[38] More telling, however, would be the work of the Spanish artist Guillem Ramos-Poqui, whose assemblages are made of what he calls "poor objects," everyday, ephemeral things (a toothbrush, a glass of water) that are staged in deliberate contrast to the surrealist object—the kinship with Ponge's relation to things, or Stein's, is worth remarking.[39] Things in this case are allowed to be (just) things, that is, proximate things. Gerald Burns says that to touch something—an object or an animal—makes the thing more like itself (TL12). My thought is that poetic things experience this kind of realization or density. As Burns says, "If the world were transparent it would be merely practical" (TL93).

Poetry exists to thicken the plot.

Conclusion

On Poems of the Third Kind (a Thought Experiment)

A poem can be a stretch of thinking.

—Barrett Watten

I've argued that poetry, or at least some modern and contemporary versions of it, is a species of conceptual art, meaning that in order to understand or even experience a piece of language (or a sound or a typographical arrangement on a page) as a poem at all, one has to be able to follow a line of thinking (or develop what performance artists call a "support language") that argues in favor of the text or event in question in spite of (or, more likely, because of) its failure to live up to the criteria or degrees of familiarity that usually help us to pick out things as poems. This raises the question of whether there can be poems in theory but not in practice, which is a question that some of the language poets have pursued in various experimental ways, opening themselves to the charge that their poems are, in fact, more theory than practice. Think, for example, of Charles Bernstein's chatty *ars poetica*, "Artifice of Absorption":

> A poetic *reading* can be given to any
> piece of writing; a "poem" may be understood as

writing specifically designed to absorb, or inflate
with, proactive—rather than reactive—styles of
reading. "Artifice" is a measure of a poem's
intractability to being read as the sum of its
devices & subject matters. In this sense,
"artifice" is the contradiction of "realism."[1]

Or recall Robert Creeley's thought in an essay titled, interestingly, "Was
that a Real Poem or Did You Just Make it Up Yourself?": "Posit that music
exists despite the possibility that no one might be consciously able to
make it, that what we call *poems* are an intrinsic fact in the human world
whether or no there be poets at this moment capable of their creation."[2]
Creeley does not go on to describe this possible state of affairs, but by
raising the possibility he imposes on us the task of doing so.

Is there a limit or test as to what a poem can or cannot be? T. S. Eliot
appealed famously to tradition, as, in his way, did Louis Zukofsky in *A
Test of Poetry*, which follows Matthew Arnold's touchstone principle of
verifying a text as poetic. I've invoked the anarchic principle that anything goes, granting the limits imposed by historical conditions, which
are limits undergoing continuous and unpredictable extension. Poetry
writing is a social practice internal to small groups with many different ways of thinking and doing things, so in principle anything can be
(somewhere, at some time) a poem. For most poetry readers, especially
in universities, this is a reprehensible principle because it denies poetry
access to the realm of universal validity formally demanded by reason,
or at least Kant's version of reason. This is a nominalist dilemma that
poetics, as a kind of philosophical discipline, is meant to address. For example, it works therapeutically as a thought experiment that measures
the strength of the criteria that we implicitly appeal to when, for instance, introducing poems into the classroom or, more flexibly perhaps,
when writing about things we call poems. Experimental poetry, or the
practice of trying out almost anything, has at least the virtue of making
us think about what concepts and arguments we would use to defend
what we think of as poetry. The honest truth is that what we think of as
reliable criteria are usually no more than habits, as when we call things

(like "Artifice of Absorption") poems because of their unjustified right-hand margins.

In defiance of this scholastic state of affairs, Gerald Burns, a poet ignored by both official verse culture and the experimentalists, once imagined a poem made of a poet adorned with random objects: "You could ask what happened to the full-tilt poem, in which you covered yourself with pinned messages, feathers, spools, things like forks balanced there, and then moved forward with it falling off you."[3] His thought seems to have been that contemporary poets have scaled down their audacity (he was thinking of Charles Olson's massive—"maximus"—projections), but he was also bringing together in a ludic way the concepts of collage, performance, and poetry's capacity for breaking its frame. Probe Burns's silliness and you find a conceptual world that is rooted in the satirical culture of Pope and Swift in which reason, offended by mechanical systems of the spirit, turns the world upside down. Burns was what I think of as a conceptual poet (who also performed as a magician and as a clown). For example, in a typically anaesthetic, antiformalist temper, he once wrote, "One can imagine a culture such that making interesting things dull is the point of art" (TL27). (Compare Robert Rauschenberg's answer, in a recent interview, to a question about what sort of photographs he likes: "I like photographs of anything uninteresting. Maybe just two doors on a wall.")[4]

Imagine, in this spirit, a *fictional* poem. A fictional poem would, by definition, not be a real one, although it would not quite be unreal either, as we know from Stephen Dedalus's "Temptress of the Villanelle," a poem that exists only in a work of fiction. To be sure, the difference between a poem in a novel and a poem in an anthology is apt to be empirically indiscernible. To speak strictly, a fictional poem would be a poem held in place less by literary history than by one of the categories that the logical world keeps in supply: conceptual models, possible worlds, speculative systems, hypothetical constructions in all of their infinite variation—or maybe just whatever finds itself caught between quotation marks, as (what we call) "reality" often is.

The French writer Maurice Blanchot, in "The Language of Fiction," introduces the concept of *irréelité* to house things that are neither real nor unreal, neither present nor absent, neither one thing nor another—Blanchot thinks of them as things of "the third kind," which he brings together under the large category of *le Neutre*. Blanchot was the first philosopher of the ontological dimension intimated by words like "almost," "not quite," "no longer," "unless," "soon," "meanwhile," and "between"—Blanchot seemed to think of it as the dimension of nonidentity. For Blanchot the basic unit of time is the interruption, whereas the basic unit of space has the shape of parentheses. Poems inhabit these temporal and spatial intervals or interstices because of what they are *not* as pieces of language. For example, poetry is not a species of speaking; it is writing (*l'écriture*) "outside of language"—that is, writing that interrupts or detours the discursive processes of nomination, predication, assertion, narration, expression, consecutive reasoning, systematic construction, and so on. It is, in Blanchot's terminology, a species of *désœuvrement:* worklessness. Its essential form is the fragment, which, speaking strictly, is not a form but an event of incompletion, a formlessness that one cannot supplement or remedy by reading.[5] Poetry, Blanchot thinks, is a species of impossibility, an event made precisely of something not happening.

In *The Captive Mind*, Czeslaw Milosz describes briefly the art of writing under totalitarian conditions, that is, in a world in which, on pain of death or worse, things cannot be said to be otherwise than they are ideologically determined to be, in other words, a rule-governed world of absolute necessity—for example, Warsaw or Prague during a certain historical period. One could also extend this to Theodor Adorno's (slightly paranoid) description of the administered world of modernity in which frictionless functioning within systematic constraints defines the norms of social existence, which is thereby almost always dysfunctional. (Kafka and Beckett were Adorno's Homer and Virgil because of their exactness in describing this dystopia.) An art of writing under captivity, Milosz says, begins as an experience of "the hunger for strangeness." Like most appetites, this is one that people keep to themselves, but it is also one that can be satisfied covertly by noticing occasions when regulations fall imperceptibly short of regularity or when some small wrinkle deforms the uniformity of the approved landscape, woodwork, or attire.[6] Writers under captive conditions have a sensibility that registers, and likewise produces, the smallest defects. For example, they learn to write "in an accepted style, terminology, and linguistic ritual," which, however, they then alter "by removing a comma, inserting an 'and,' establishing this rather than another sequence in the problems discussed."[7] This alteration constitutes a work of art. Under these circumstances one could write a poem by arbitrarily leaving a word out of a document that one is required to compose according to form. The poem in this event would be made of a word not written; it would be a text with a hole through which perhaps all the rest of its words drain away. In this sense, Milosz has given us one way of interpreting or applying Blanchot's poetics.[8]

(Recall the modern, and indeed contemporary, practice of composing a poem by erasing or altering words, lines, or whole portions of the texts of canonical works. [See below.] Or think of John Cage's "mesostics" in which he "writes through" the great works of modernism like Pound's *Cantos* and Joyce's *Finnegans Wake*.)

In years past, linguists and others have pictured language as being under the constraint of rules and procedures, deep structures as well as conventional forms of usage, including those supposed to govern poetry writing, if only locally, periodically, controversially, or according to some conceptual improvising. However, one can also imagine a language in which rules do not descend all the way to the bottom—a *nomadic* language, as Gilles Deleuze and Felix Guattari use this term, a language made of variables in a perpetual state of variation.[9] It is not difficult to imagine a poem as the product of a language not working as intended, not taking dictation but, say, punning, as languages do when not carefully policed. Jacques Derrida, for example, thinks of philosophy as a world in which puns are forbidden, and philosophers are those who monitor our uses of language to make sure that nothing is said that is not intended, justified, or at least plausible.[10] Habermas confirms this idea in spectacular fashion by instituting philosophers as "guardians of rationality" whose task is to keep poetic language—language used for its own sake—from infiltrating the public realm of problem-solving speech acts, whose norm is the propositional style of philosophical discourse.[11] Deleuze and Guattari think of language as made of "order-words," that is, expressions of command and obedience, affirmation and negation, petition and gratitude. Language is imperative, a top-down structure of power and obligation in which nothing is expressed except utterances agreed on in advance. A poem under this regime would be simply what cannot be said. In these theories no one thing counts as language, but only events of speech controlled by historical and cultural disciplines of the kind Foucault describes in his *Order of Discourse*—rarefactions of language designed to reduce what can be said to the rational, the true, or the authorized. We can imagine a poem as discourse rarefied to abstraction, perhaps one of Paul Celan's last poems:

ST
Ein Vau, pf, in der That,
Schlägt, mps,
o
oo
ooo
O[12]

A kind of hyperbole informs these poststructuralist thoughts (otherwise they would be without much interest). More to the point for the possibilities of poetry would be Donald Davidson's pragmatic conception of language as a "passing theory" got up on the spot to cope with what someone might be saying at any given moment, as when Mrs. Malaprop gives her ingenious twists to what words mean. A "passing theory" is an improvised revision of what Davidson calls a "prior theory," namely the sort of practical know-how that enables us to understand the speech of others even when that speech defies or deforms the formal properties of intelligible speech. A "prior theory" is roughly what Noam Chomsky would mean by linguistic competence, but for Davidson that competence is rooted in experience rather than in rules. A "passing theory" enables us to understand linguistic incompetence, which we do routinely. Davidson refers us to Mrs. Malaprop, but sometimes in place of malapropisms he substitutes Joyce's *Finnegans Wake*. His idea is that in order to understand malapropisms and Wakean neologisms we need to construct, on the spur of the moment, a "passing theory" of how these words work and what is meant by them—in other words, we have to reinvent our English, revise or reconstruct the "prior theory," in order to understand what is said as "English" *in this particular instance*, however bizarre. Of course, this means that there is no such thing as "English," only "passing theories" of English that enable us to accommodate broken English, Yorkshire dialects, slangs, argots, word salads, translations from Japanese, teen-age passwords, glossolalia, and much of what passes for poetry. Davidson is fairly straightforward about this: "I conclude that there is no such thing as a language, not if a language is anything like what many philosophers and linguists have supposed." Language is not made of universals; on the contrary, "a feature of the concept of language as I have described it is that there must be an infinity of 'languages' no one has ever spoken or ever will."[13] Contrary to Chomsky's viewpoint, linguistic competence means the ability to dispense with rules.

In Davidson's pragmatic theory, every poem is a language unto itself, each one entailing its own "passing theory"—hence, the idea of poetry as conceptual art. Even more interesting is what follows from Davidson's conclusion that "there must be an infinity of 'languages' no one has ever spoken or ever will." We could, without penalty or guilt, substitute "poems" for "languages," in which case we could imagine a possible world, or perhaps a culture, in which the nonexistence of a poem could not be counted against its being a poem. What Davidson has in mind seems to me vaguely Parmenidean: Anything that is possible exists. What is actual is merely local, that is, internal to the world we happen to inhabit. To actualize something is simply to bring it into our present context.

Jorie Graham's poems in *Materialism* are "adaptations" from texts like Bacon's *Novum Organum*, Dante's *Inferno*, essays by Walter Benjamin, and Brecht's "A Short Organum for the Theater." Adaptation, Graham notes, means that the source text has been "edited, rewritten in spots, or assembled out of fragments from the larger work named."[14] It can also mean that the source is simply reproduced verbatim: The poem "from Wittgenstein's *Tractatus*," for example, excerpts, without altering, propositions 2.026 ("There must be objects, if the world is to have an unalterable form") through 2.063 ("The sum total of reality is the world") of the original text. The implicit claim here is that the text of any genre is either already a poem or can be made into one simply by deleting some of its parts and moving some other parts around, reconstructing bits and pieces into new arrangements. Graham's poetics in *Materialism* recalls the ancient rhetorical/theatrical practice known as "travesty," and indeed one can think of her book as a form of comic or satirical writing.

Conceptually, however, *Materialism* raises the question of what counts as language—the Chomskyan language that each of us learns and uses according to the rules of linguistic competence or the Davidsonian language that presupposes something like a vast library similar to the one Jorge Luis Borges imagined in "The Library of Babel"? According to the narrator of that story, the words I am writing now could be found in one of the library's indefinite number of volumes that contain all possible combinations and permutations of some twenty-odd orthographical symbols. In such a case, to write would simply be, as in Graham's plagiarism of Wittgenstein's propositions, a form of recitation, recontextualization, or rhetorical invention—an act ultimately of *finding* a text rather than producing an original one. In transplanting Wittgenstein's propositions, Graham is giving application to the *modernist* poetics of the "found object." To exhibit a found object is to "objectify" it, as if enclosing it in a frame. Graham's excerpt from the *Tractatus* invisibly alters the original in the same way Duchamp alters an ordinary snow shovel by transplanting it from a hardware store to his studio. And in a further turn of the screw, she is also posing a philosophical problem comparable or perhaps even identical to the one posed by Borges in his story "Pierre Menard, Author of Don Quixote": "He [Menard] did not want to compose another *Don Quixote*—which would be easy—but *the Don Quixote*. It is unnecessary to add that his aim was never to produce a mechanical transcription of the original; he did not propose to copy it. His admirable ambition was to produce pages which would coincide—word for word and line for line—with those of Miguel de Cervantes."[15] Blanchot would see in Graham's "adaptation," as in Menard's achievement, the construction of a "poem of the third kind," neither original nor merely a reproduction but hanging forever in between the two orders of existence. A final point would be that Graham is, in fact, glossing

Wittgenstein's thesis that "There must be objects, if the world is to have an unalterable form," because what she produces in her "adaptation" is a piece of the world in its unaltered and unalterable form.

In contrast to Jorie Graham's practice of adapting high-culture texts, ascending as she does even to Plato's *Phaedo,* poets like Karen Mac Cormack and Alan Halsey expropriate texts from popular culture: newspapers, magazines, advertisements—in other words, the language that circulates in our everyday commercial, mass-produced, electronic, and now digital environment. In *At Issue* Karen Mac Cormack uses "the vocabulary and spelling found in magazines of a diverse nature," a practice she calls "mining." The mined texts are "health/fitness magazines" aimed at a female audience, and recomposed, they produce poems like this extract:

At Issue III

Putting shape into getting without perfect in a culture that doesn't think, pumps up, the two traits go at the face of rate themselves, cropped by impasse, express your monochromatics from within, discover it blushes, reduce the signs to surface, sharing space in a new high-tech fabric, the pale face extra-prevent every day year after year, retreat returns by filling out advance notice, since seeing is oxygen more supple, sways, just take graceful, tilt feature-controls are big, stable rattles accept different speeds sing, sprawl moguls seized a story, raking in celebrity, heat-activated genre, hands full turned.[16]

We could read this poem as a critique of poetic diction: What sorts of words are allowed into a poem? In the eighteenth century the circle inscribed for *poetical* words was fairly small. Even Gerard Manley Hopkins thought that words like "duck" and "potato" could not be admitted into a poem. Karen Mac Cormack's poem, precisely because of its paratactic arrangement of words, puts certain keywords of popular culture on exhibit—one has no trouble picking them out (the main thesis is "to get into shape"). *At Issue* "stages" the language of our cultural environment and, as such, "defamiliarizes" it, that is, situates it in the enabling condition of art, where, as said, anything goes.

In 1966 the artist Dan Graham began circulating texts under the name *Schema March 1966*, each one of which was a version of the other, each one composed more or less as follows:

1	adjectives
3	adverbs
1192½ sq. ems.	area not occupied by type
337½ sq. ems.	area occupied by type
1	columns
0	conjunctions
nil	depression of type into surface of page
0	gerunds
0	infinitives
363	letters of the alphabet
27	lines
2	mathematical symbols
38	nouns
52	numbers
0	participles
8½ × 5	page
17½ × 22½	paper sheet
offset cartridge	paper stock
5	prepositions
0	pronouns
10 pt.	type size
Press Roman	typeface
59	words
2	words capitalized
0	words italicized
57	words not capitalized
0	words not italicized

This self-referential poem lists the verbal, graphic, and material elements of which it would be composed when composed, although it is, of course, already a composition, however schematic. Call it an "in-between" or, better, a merely conceptual poem that can only be actualized by following its recipe, filling in the generic lines and materials with specific or actual ones. But is there any reason not to think of it as already a poem unto itself, one made of the words that schematize a form into which many poems could be made to fit? Think of it as a poem in advance of any number of poems—a true avant-garde work of art, a poem machine. In this respect it is perhaps no different from any generic form—the sonnet, for example: It is a structure into which any words might be inserted.

I could certainly produce more examples of poetry that reconceptualizes itself in the process of being composed. The history of poetry is a history of the reconceptualization of poetry—and of language as well. If poetry has a purpose, it is to keep history—and not just its own—from coming to an end. Arguably we could even make ourselves into poems by developing practices of reinvention—a practice encouraged by Michel Foucault in his last writings, where he argues that because the self is not a given, not something we possess in the nature of things, "we have to create ourselves as a work of art."[17]

Notes

Abbreviations

P   Zukofsky, *Prepositions+*
PM   McCaffery, *Prior to Meaning*
S   Cage, *Silence*
TD   Artaud, *The Theater and Its Double*
TL   Burns, *A Thing about Language*

Introduction. An Apology for Poetry

1. Quoted in Sharp, "Lawrence Weiner at Amsterdam," 71.

2. Conceptual art is often said to be art that raises the question of what counts as art, as when Marcel Duchamp installs an ordinary object such as a snow shovel in his studio and declares it to be his latest composition. All by itself this is at most a dada gesture, but it poses a serious philosophical problem (perhaps the fundamental problem of *modernism*), because it lowers the threshold of what could count as art to degree zero, in which case logically nothing can be excluded from being art—a condition of nominalism that no one but an anarchist (like me) could be happy with. Moreover, as if in response to this problem, Duchamp's gesture entails a complex network of concepts that could (and should) be spelled out by way of argument or consecutive reasoning. For example, his Readymade is a repudiation of the (high) culture of the museum and a rejection of the *Grand Œuvre* as a knockdown answer to the question of what counts as art. It is an

instance of the aesthetics of the "found object." It is an instance of figuration, that is, a transformation of the plain or literal by recontextualizing it, placing it in a strange situation (defamiliarization, Brechtian *Verfremdungseffekt*, or the Russian formalist's *Ostrenenie*): The work of art becomes the product of what is logically a category mistake, which is how metaphor works. Further, it proposes a theory of exhibition aesthetics: Put an ordinary object on a platform, stage, or inside a framed space, and it ceases to be ordinary without ceasing to be the thing it is—thus raising the philosophical problem of indiscernibles that Arthur Danto investigates in *The Transfiguration of the Commonplace*. Duchamp *theatricalizes* the snow shovel—an event that in turn raises once more the question of what counts as theater. One could extend these lines of thought in various directions. It is the nature of conceptual art to cause precisely this sort of open-ended thinking. See Alberro and Stimson's indispensable sourcebook *Conceptual Art*, which contains just about every important critical essay on the subject, including Joseph Kosuth's famous essay "Art after Philosophy" (158–77) and the inaugural editorial of *Art and Language*, which introduces the concept of conceptual art by asking whether it (the editorial itself) could "come up for the count" as a piece of art (101).

3. Auden, "Caliban to the Audience," 112; Crane, "General Aims and Theories," 21.

4. Mac Cormack, *Quill Driver*, 48.

5. Wittgenstein, *Philosophical Investigations*, § 67–71.

6. See MacIntyre, *Whose Justice? Which Rationality?* esp. 355. See also MacIntyre, *Three Rival Versions of Moral Inquiry*, esp. 150.

7. Retallack, *How to Do Things with Words*, 43.

8. Reference is to Jorge Guitart, "Trakl, Yo No Se Aleman," *Foreigner's Notebook* (Buffalo, N.Y.: Shuffaloff Books, 1993).

9. Reference is to Jackson Mac Low, *42 Merzgedichte in Memoriam Kurt Schwitters: February 1987–September 1989* (Barrytown, N.Y.: Station Hill Press, 1994).

10. Perloff, "After Free Verse: The New Nonlinear Poetries," in *Poetry on and off the Page*, esp. 157–67.

11. See, for example, Silliman, "Disappearance of the Word, Appearance of the World" (1977), 121–32.

12. Danto, "Art and Disturbation," in *Philosophical Disenfranchisement of Art*.

13. Bernstein, "Artifice of Absorption," 65.

14. See McCaffery, "Writing as a General Economy," in *North of Intention*, esp. 213–15. Behind this essay stands the work of the French writer Georges Bataille, esp. "The Notion of Expenditure" (1933). "Gratuitous expenditure" means pure outlay with no return on investment, as when words are spoken but not exchanged for meaning. The term refers to what Bataille calls "the principle of loss." Bataille writes: "The term poetry, applied to the least degraded and least intellectual forms of the expression of the state of loss, can be considered synonymous with expenditure; it in fact signifies, in the most precise way, creation by means of loss. Its meaning is therefore close to that of *sacrifice*" (120).

15. Spicer, "After Lorca," 33–34.

16. See Levinas, "Language and Proximity," esp. 118. See also Bruns, "Concepts of Art and Poetry in Emmanuel Levinas's Writings."

17. Quoted in McCaffery, "The Elsewhere of Meaning," in *North of Intention*, 171.

18. Ibid. See Drucker, "Visual Performance of the Poetic Text," esp. 147–56. Iliazd also edited an anthology of early twentieth-century experimental poetry, *Poésie de mots inconnu.*

19. McCaffery, *North of Intention*, 175.

One. Poetry as an Event of Language: The Conceptual Achievement of Contemporary Poetics

1. Nussbaum, "Flawed Crystals" (the essay first appeared in *New Literary History* in 1983); MacIntyre, *After Virtue*; Rorty, "Heidegger, Kundera, and Dickens"; Danto, "Literature and/as Philosophy," in *Philosophical Disenfranchisement of Art*; Cavell, *Disowning Knowledge in Six Plays of Shakespeare.*

2. See the Chicago critic Elder Olson's argument to this effect in "Outline of Poetic Theory," 564.

3. Rorty, "Heidegger, Kundera, and Dickens," 69–70.

4. Fisher, "Poetics of the Complexity Manifold."

5. In fairness to Rorty and the rest one could just as well put the question of poetry to literary professors, whose interest in poetry, at least since the decline of the New Criticism (in other words, for the past fifty years), has been fairly scattered. In fact, the "marginalization of poetry" is now a kind of after-dinner topic in literary studies. See, for example, Bob Perelman's "The Marginalization of Poetry," a poem read at a conference devoted to the theme of the marginalization of poetry. Recently Jonathan Culler, in his valedictory address as retiring president

of the American Comparative Literature Association, observed that "Poetry was once central to literary experience, and the consideration of the nature of the lyric—or poetic language—was once central to theory. This is no longer the case. When literature is important for theory, it comes in the guise of narrative." Interestingly, Culler first made this observation some twenty years ago. But his question still seems current: Why this ascendancy of narrative? Culler's suggestion is that "in an age of critical demystification [the new historicism, cultural studies, postcolonial studies, psychoanalytic criticism] poetry seems embarrassing. Theorists can make claims about the fundamental importance of fictional narrative to the construction of the subject, to desire and identity, to the imagined communities that are nations, and so on. It's harder to imagine making such claims about the lyric." After all, narrative has to do with real things, whereas lyric gives voice to an experience of private transport that condenses the world and the poet—and the reader—into "an eternal *now*." "The abjection of lyric," Culler says, "has been a condition of theory's self-constitution." Abjection is a good choice of words: The abject is what the physical or social body must evacuate in order to keep itself healthy or whole. To keep literary studies on message we abject the lyric and confine poetics to a museum housing Aristotle, Horace, Sidney, Wordsworth, and so on. See Culler, "Comparing Poetry," esp. ix–xi.

6. Quoted by Simic, *Metaphysician in the Dark*, 46.

7. Strand, *The Continuous Life*, 61–62.

8. Mallarmé, "The Book, a Spiritual Instrument," 24.

9. Langbaum, *The Poetry of Experience*.

10. Bell, *Book of the Dead Man*, 43.

11. Ibid., 41.

12. See, however, chapter 1, note 16, and also Perloff, *Twenty-first-Century Modernism*, esp. chapter 5, "'Modernism' at the Millennium," which shows the continuity of language-centered writing from Gertrude Stein and the early Eliot through much of contemporary poetry. Perloff's book is a persuasive argument against the "end-of-history" theories of (post)modernism.

13. Coolidge, *The Maintains*, 1.

14. Bernstein, "Maintaining Space: Clark Coolidge's Early Works," in *Content's Dream*, 261.

15. Stein, *Writings and Lectures*, 172–73. See Quartermain, *Disjunctive Poetics*.

16. See Andrews and Bernstein, eds., *The L=A=N=G=U=A=G=E Book*,

which reprints the first three volumes of the journal *L=A=N=G=U=A=G=E*, which Andrews and Bernstein edited between 1978 and 1981; Bernstein, ed., *43 Poets (1984)*; Silliman, ed., *In the American Tree*; Messerli, ed., *Language Poetries*; and Perloff, "The Word as Such: L=A=N=G=U=A=G=E Writing in the Eighties," in *Dance of the Intellect*. A now-classic account of the turn against the principle of integration is the poet Ron Silliman's "The New Sentence," in *The New Sentence*.

17. See Perloff, *Dance of the Intellect*, esp. chapters 7 and 8, "From Image to Action: The Return of Story in Postmodern Poetry" and "Postmodernism and the Impasse of the Lyric." For a radical reconceptualization of narrative as a literary form, see McCaffery and Nichol, "Report 2."

18. See Silliman, "Disappearance of the Word, Appearance of the World." For a more recent account of formal experiments in recent poetry, see Waldrop, "Form and Discontent."

19. Bernstein, "Artifice of Absorption," 73.

20. McCaffery, *Seven Pages Missing*, 1:292.

21. McCaffery, "The Kommunist Manifesto, or Wot We Wukkerz Want," in *Seven Pages Missing*, 2:171. One can hear McCaffery give a rendering of this translation in the first of his *LINE-break* interviews with Charles Bernstein. See his Web site at the Electronic Poetry Center (http://epc.buffalo.edu/authors/mccaffery/).

22. McCaffery, *Seven Pages Missing*, 2:359.

23. Coolidge, "Arrangement," in *Talking Poetics from Naropa Institute*, 159–60.

24. On the relationship between the figure of the mineral world and Coolidge's conception of poetic language, see Ziarek, "Word for Sign."

25. Coolidge, *Talking Poetics from Naropa Institute*, 144.

26. Palmer, ed., *Code of Signals*, 178.

27. Watten, "Total Syntax," 61.

28. Ibid., 51.

29. Burns, A *Thing about Language* (hereafter TL), 60.

30. See McCaffery, "*The Martyrology* as Paragram," in *North of Intention*. A paragram is a text whose letters and phonemes form networks of signification independently of the grammatical forms of phrase structures, sentences, and paragraphs. The term derives from Kristeva, "Pour une sémiologie des paragrammes."

31. Burns, "The Slate Notebook," 26.

32. Hejinian, *The Language of Inquiry*, 44. One can read this essay as a response to Fredric Jameson's famous criticism of language poetry as "schizophrenic," mere word salad or fragmentation. See Jameson, *Postmodernism*, 26.

33. Hejinian, *The Language of Inquiry*, 44.

34. Ibid., 43.

35. Gadamer, *Truth and Method*, 110.

36. Ibid., 116.

37. Ibid., 134.

38. Ibid., 122.

39. Hejinian, *The Language of Inquiry*, 27.

40. Ibid., 27–28.

41. See Perloff, "Language Poetry and the Lyric Subject," 405–34.

42. Bernstein, "The Revenge of the Poet-Critic; or The Parts are Greater than the Sum of the Whole," in *My Way*, 9.

43. Bernstein, *Republics of Reality*, 13–14.

44. Bernstein, *My Way*, 25.

45. Bernstein, *Dark City*, 85–89.

46. Ibid., 94.

47. Online advertisement for *2004 Poet's Market: 1800 Places to Publish Your Poetry* (New York: Writer's Digest Books, 2004), available at the Writers Store (www.writersstore.com/product.php?products_id=338), accessed May 28, 2004.

48. Bakhtin, *The Dialogic Imagination*, 296.

49. Bernstein, *My Way*, 10.

50. Bernstein, *Content's Dream*, 38.

51. DuPlessis, *The Pink Guitar*, 155. See McGann, *Black Riders*, 143: "poetry is that form of discourse whose only object is to allow language to display itself, to show how it lives. . . . [Poetry] is language practicing itself."

52. Retallack, *Afterrimages*, 24.

53. See Marion, *In Excess*, 54–81.

54. See Marion, *Crossing of the Visible*, esp. 14–19.

Two. The Transcendence of Words: A Short Defense of (Sound) Poetry

1. McCaffery, *Prior to Meaning* (hereafter PM).

2. MacIntyre, *Whose Justice? Which Rationality?*

3. Levinas, *Otherwise than Being*, 114.

4. William Carlos Williams, *Imaginations*, 59.

5. Ibid.

6. Ibid., 70.

7. See Fredric Jameson's discussion of this issue in connection with Theodor Adorno's aesthetic theory, *Late Marxism*, 157–64.

8. Cavell, *The Senses of Walden*, 135.

9. Levinas, "Language and Proximity," 118.

10. Levinas, *The Levinas Reader*, 147.

11. Ibid.

12. Novarina, *Theater of the Ears*, esp. 42–61 ("Letter to the Actors"). See Kahn and Whitehead, eds., *Wireless Imagination*, which contains a valuable essay on German *hörspiele* by Mark E. Cory, "Soundplay: The Polyphonous Tradition of German Radio Art."

13. The classical argument to this effect is in an essay on "The Artworld" in which the philosopher and art critic Arthur Danto tries to defend as art Andy Warhol's pop art, specifically his *Brillo Boxes*, which are, with some qualifications, indiscernible from actual Brillo boxes, raising the question of whether a real thing can be a work of art (as if a work of art were not a real thing). Danto's words are worth citing: "What in the end makes the difference between a Brillo Box and a work of art consisting of a Brillo Box is a certain theory of art. It is the theory that takes it up into the world of art, and keeps it from collapsing into the real object which it is (in a sense of is other than that of artistic identification). Of course, without the theory, one is unlikely to see it as art, and in order to see it as part of the artworld, one must have mastered a good deal of artistic theory as well as a considerable amount of the history of recent New York painting. It could not have been art fifty years ago. But then there could not have been, everything being equal, flight insurance in the Middle Ages, or Etruscan typewriter erasers. The world has to be ready for such things, the artworld no less than the real one. It is the role of artistic theories, these days as always, to make the artworld, or art, possible" (581).

14. Zukofsky, "A Statement for Poetry," in *Prepositions +* (hereafter P), 20.

15. Cage, "History of Experimental Music in the United States" (1958), in *Silence* (hereafter S), 72.

16. Levinas, *The Levinas Reader*, 148.

17. My friend Marjorie Perloff has cautioned me about Cage's assertion that the composer "gives up control." In his compositions and events, Cage is certainly in charge—but he is in charge less like the author of a plot than like the

instigator of a riot. The idea is to set things in motion without arranging for their development.

18. For a counterstatement to everything I have said (and will say), see Siegmund Levarie's essay "Noise." In the essay Levarie begins with a distinction between disorderly sound (noise) and orderly sound (tone). The outer world is made of noise, whereas "tone is an accomplishment" of civilization (22). Mere sound is inherently threatening, but "tone" is redemptive: "This association between sound and the threatening outer world, early established, lies within the everyday experience of all of us. Our mature differentiation between noise and tone has a bearing on our enjoyment of listening to music. For while we remain defenseless before the power of any sound, the controlled presentation of orderly tones in a good composition obviates the primeval threat. The intelligible organization of music permits us to master and subsequently enjoy the otherwise confusing and often irritating acoustical stimuli. Noise, on the other hand, evokes in adults and children alike a direct reflex action as if it were a signal of danger, or an unpleasant attack. Indicative in this regard is our immediate reaction, without interference of logical thought, to thunder and lightning. Although we know that lightning may ignite our house and kill us, we really shudder, not at the dangerous flash, but at the accompanying noise of the harmless thunder" (23–24). Naturally Levarie deplores the turn toward dissonance in music since Arnold Schoenberg (30). He doesn't mention John Cage, but he clearly has him in mind when he denounces "the new barbarianism, with its premusical, precivilized worship of noise, glissando, and indistinct pitches[, which] offers no vision and denies natural and artistic norms. It is like screaming during a catastrophe—an occupation that is neither musical nor artful. The responsible reaction is to try to recognize noise for what it is and to assess it accordingly" (31). A sound poet would, however, appreciate Levarie's observation that "all consonants are noises, and all vowels are tones" (22).

19. See also Higgins, "Early Sound Poetry" and "The Golem in the Text," in *Modernism since Postmodernism*.

20. Versions of the essay are also available in Bernstein, ed., *Close Listening*, and Morris, ed., *Sound States*, but the essay has had many incarnations. See, for example, "Sound Poetry: A Survey," in McCaffrey and Nichol, eds., *Sound Poetry*, which served as the catalog for the Eleventh International Sound Poetry Festival, Toronto, Canada, October 14–17, 1978.

21. See Charles Olson, "Projective Verse."

22. Kostelanetz, "Text-Sound Art: A Survey," in Kostelanetz, ed., *Text-Sound Texts*, 14.

23. The British poet Tom Raworth is interesting for the way he turns a poetry reading into a sound performance by reading his poems as fast as he can. Most famous in this regard is perhaps *Ace*, a long poem whose lines consist at most of only three or four words, more often one or two, thus making the poem much more difficult to read quickly than if it were printed as prose, as Tom Orange points out in a very fine essay "Notes for a Reading of *Ace*."

24. Douglas Kahn's important book *Noise, Water, Meat*, esp. 260–89, provides a useful passage on immersion as an avant-garde experience. Interestingly, Kahn doesn't take up contemporary sound poetry.

25. Mac Low, *Representative Works*, 251.

26. Ibid., 280. Compare Steve McCaffery on the sound-poetry group the Four Horsemen: "Ours is an art of intensities and change, of rapid passages into and out of cohesion, incohesion, deterritorializations and territorialities. It is the art of transition, of displacements at thresholds and passages in and out of recognitions. Ad hoc arrival points tend to lend structure to the pieces. . . . The question of arrival through aleatoric and spontaneous perambulations involves the issue of knowing when a destination is reached. The key to . . . how we know where we are, how we know that we'll get there . . . is embedded in ecouture—a kind of developed expertise in the aural. We've trained ourselves to be good listeners and sensitive barometers to each other. This I believe is the crucial thing in our performance, for without the listening, without that awareness of the energy states of each other the knowingness would be impossible" ("Discussion . . . Genesis . . . Continuity," 277).

27. McCaffery, *North of Intention*, 152–55.

28. Deleuze and Guattari, *A Thousand Plateaus*, 76. See Debord, "All the King's Men," esp. 114: "The problem of language is at the heart of all struggles between the forces striving to abolish the present alienation and those striving to maintain it; it is inseparable from the entire terrain of those struggles. We live within language as within polluted air. In spite of what the humorists think, words do not play. . . . Words *work*—on behalf of the dominant organization of life. And yet they are not completely automatized; unfortunately for the theoreticians of information, words are not in themselves 'informationist'; they embody forces that can upset the most careful calculations. Words coexist with power in a relationship analogous to that which proletarians . . . have with

power. Employed *almost* constantly, exploited full time for every sense and non-sense that can be squeezed out of them, they still remain fundamentally strange and foreign." And the task of poetry, Debord goes on to argue, is to intensify and exaggerate this foreignness. Poetry is the insubordination of language: "Power's stranglehold over language is similar to its stranglehold over the totality. Only a language that has been deprived of all immediate reference to the totality can serve as the basis for information. Information is the poetry of power, the counterpoetry of law and order, the mediated falsification of what exists. Conversely, poetry must be understood as immediate communication within reality and as real alteration of reality. It is nothing other than liberated language . . . , language which breaks its rigid significations and simultaneously embraces words, music, cries, gestures, painting, mathematics, facts, acts" (115).

29. Chopin, "Why I Am the Author of Free and Sound Poetry." Available at the UbuWeb site (www.ubuweb.com/papers/chopin.html). Last accessed April 19, 2004.

30. Artaud, *Theater and Its Double* (hereafter TD), 89. See also McCaffery, *Prior to Meaning:* "Chopin's notorious splicings and layerings organize the temporal appearance of the sonic like a writing. It would be inaccurate, however, to represent him as an exponent of a strictly secondary orality. Admittedly, he has recorded his works extensively and used technology to realize an impressive and definable audiographics. Such work bears all the characteristics of a graphism: iterability, retrievability, and replication. Chopin's primary concern in his use of tape, however, is to extend the parameters of performance. If the quotidian impact of audiotechnologies has been the permanent separation of speech from a present subject (via radio, the telephone, and the gramophone), then we must credit Chopin for repossessing vocality as a new nonsemantic lexicon, a material modified, purified of the Logos and then returned to a performative, gestural poetics" (PM179).

31. See Jean-François Lyotard's argument in favor of a "theater of energies" against one of meanings, "La dent, la paume."

32. See Michel Foucault's "Discourse on Language," esp. 216–20. See also the interview with Foucault "Truth and Power," esp. 131.

33. Waldenfels, "The Ruled and the Unruly," 192.

34. See Foucault, "The Abnormals," 51–57.

35. McCaffery, *Seven Pages Missing*, 2:362.

36. See Bruns, "Towards a Hermeneutics of Freedom," 247–66.

37. See Kenner, *The Stoic Comedians*, esp. 37–50 (on "the book as book"); and

Ong, S.J., "System, Space, and Intellect in Renaissance Symbolism," 68–87, esp. 74–77.

38. See the anthology edited by Jed Rasula and Steve McCaffery, *Imagining Language*.

39. Perhaps the typewriter is not so modest, according to Friedrich Kittler in *Gramophone, Film, Typewriter*. See also Hayles, *Writing Machines*.

40. Gomringer, "From Line to Constellation," 67.

41. Citation is from McCaffery's unpaginated introduction to *Carnival*. See Perloff, "Inner Tension / In Attention: Steve McCaffery's Book Art," in *Poetry on and off the Page*, 264–89.

42. Kenner, *Poetry of Ezra Pound*, 215.

43. Pound, *The Pisan Cantos*, LXXIV, 22–23.

44. Charles Olson, "Projective Verse," 57.

45. Charles Bernstein prefers to describe Pound's "page" as a form of montage rather than collage. The one juxtaposes incongruous materials "in the service of one unifying theme," whereas in the other there is no totality, only singularities. This is true if one grasps *The Cantos* as a totality, something I've never been able to do, but it seems to me that one still experiences the typography of the page as a simultaneity, not as a seriality (as in montage). See Bernstein, "Pound and the Poetry of Today," in *My Way*, 161–62. See also 203–10 of the same for an illuminating discussion of seriality in Charles Reznikoff's poetry.

46. See Bruns, "Mallarmé: The Transcendence of Language and the Aesthetics of the Book," in *Modern Poetry and the Idea of Language*, 101–37, esp. 115.

47. Kenner, *The Pound Era*, 90. See also Kenner, "Pound Typing."

48. Drucker, *The Visible Word*, 168–192.

49. The Noigandres group borrowed the term "verbovocovisual" from Joyce's *Finnegans Wake*. See Perloff, "Concrete Prose."

50. Solt, ed., *Concrete Poetry*, 106. See Solt, ed., also for Augusto and Haroldo de Campos's "Pilot Plan for Concrete Poetry": "Ideogram: appeal to nonverbal communication. Concrete poem communicates its own structure: structure-content. Concrete poem is an object in and by itself, not an interpreter of exterior objects and/or more or less subjective feelings. Its material: word (sound, visual form, semantical charge). Its problem: a problem of functions-relations of this material. Factors of proximity and similitude, gestalt psychology. Rhythm: relational force. Concrete poem, by using the phonetical system (digits) and analogical syntax, creates a specific linguistic area—'*verbovocovisual*'—which shares the advantages of nonverbal communication without giving up word's

virtualities. With the concrete poem occurs the phenomenon of metacommunication: coincidence and simultaneity; only—it must be noted—it deals with a communication of forms, of a structure-content, not with the usual message of communication" (71–72).

51. Kostelanetz, *Text-Sound Texts*, 58.

52. See Craig Dworkin's study of the visuality of poetry, *Reading the Illegible*, esp. 50–87.

53. Solt, ed., *Concrete Poetry*, 78.

54. Öyvind Fahlström, "Nyarsklockorna" (1954), a permutational poem, in Emmett Williams, ed., *Anthology of Concrete Poetry*, n.p.

55. Solt, ed., *Concrete Poetry*, 76.

56. Kac, "Holopoetry, Hypertext, Hyperpoetry," 74.

57. See, for example, Cayley, "Hypertext/Cybertext/Poetext."

58. See Ikonen, "Moving Text in Avant-Garde Poetry."

Three. Poetic Materialism: The Poet's Redemption of Everyday Things

1. See Brown, *A Sense of Things*.

2. Pound, *Selected Poems*, 35.

3. Pound, *Literary Essays of Ezra Pound*, 3.

4. William Carlos Williams, *Paterson*, 14–15.

5. William Carlos Williams, *Imaginations*, 150.

6. Ibid., 117.

7. Ibid., 102.

8. William Carlos Williams, "Pastoral," 17.

9. Bruns, *Modern Poetry and the Idea of Language*.

10. Ponge, *Le parti pris des choses, suive de Proêmes*, 176.

11. Ponge, *Selected Poems*, 17.

12. Ponge, "L'Objet, c'est la poétique," in *The Power of Language*, 46–47.

13. Gavronsky, "Interview with Francis Ponge," 3.

14. Ponge, "Introduction au Galet," in *The Power of Language*, 77–78.

15. Ponge, *The Power of Language*, 112.

16. Ibid., 113.

17. See Ponge, *The Making of the Pré*, 35.

18. Ponge, "Introduction au Galet," in *The Power of Language*, 77–78.

19. Ponge, *Le parti pris des choses, suive de Proêmes*, 44.

20. Ponge, *Selected Poems*, 29.

21. Ponge, *Le parti pris des choses, suive de Proêmes*, 53–54.

22. Ponge, *Selected Poems*, 43–44.

23. Gavronsky, "Interview with Francis Ponge," 37.

24. See Silliman, "Z-Sited Path," in *The New Sentence*; and Palmer, "On Objectivism." And see especially Fredman, *A Minora for Athena*, esp. 117–51.

25. See "An Objective" (P12–18) and "Sincerity and Objectification, with Special Reference to the Work of Charles Reznikoff," (P193–202). See also Bernstein, "Reznikoff's Nearness," in *My Way*, esp. 210–21.

26. Marjorie Perloff's work has clarified this distinction in definitive ways. See, for example, "Pound/Stevens: Whose Era?" in Perloff, *Dance of the Intellect*, esp. 21–23.

27. Levinas, "Language and Proximity," 118.

28. Zukofsky, *Complete Short Poetry*, 326.

29. See Strauss, "Approaching *80 Flowers*."

30. Gertrude Stein, *Writings and Lectures*, 125–26.

31. Ibid., 115.

32. Heidegger, *Being and Time*, 98–99.

33. Brown, *A Sense of Things*, p. 74.

34. Burns, *Shorter Poems*, 100–101.

35. Ibid., 3.

36. Burns, *Shorter Poems*, 55–56.

37. See Tim Travis, "Strange Attraction."

38. See Simic, *Dime-Store Alchemy*.

39. See Ramos-Poqui's Web site, www.ramos-poqui.com, which contains a brief account of his exhibition of assemblages in 1968 at the Arts Laboratory in Drury Lane.

Conclusion. On Poems of the Third Kind (a Thought Experiment)

1. Bernstein, "Artifice of Absorption," 9.

2. Creeley, *Was That a Real Poem*, 103.

3. Burns, "Scale and Interest" (TL65).

4. Rauschenberg, interview, 13.

5. I try to clarify Blanchot's poetics in my book *Maurice Blanchot*.

6. Milosz, *The Captive Mind*, 67.

7. Ibid., 78–79.

8. See also Leo Strauss's *Persecution and the Art of Writing*.

9. Deleuze and Guattari, "1227: Treatise on Nomadology—the War Machine," in A *Thousand Plateaus*.

10. Derrida, "Proverb," 18.

11. Habermas, "Philosophy as Stand-in and Interpreter," 17.

12. Paul Celan, *Dritter Band*, 136.

13. Davidson, "A Nice Derangement of Epitaphs," 174. See my essay, "Donald Davidson among the Outcasts."

14. Jorie Graham, *Materialism*, 145.

15. Jorge Luis Borges, *Ficciones*, trans. Anthony Kerrigan (New York: Grove Press, 1962), 48–49.

16. Mac Cormack, *At Issue*, 9, 17.

17. Foucault, "On the Genealogy of Ethics," 262.

Bibliography

Alberro, Alexander, and Blake Stimson, eds. *Conceptual Art: A Critical Anthology*. Cambridge, Mass.: MIT Press, 1999.

Andrews, Bruce, and Charles Bernstein, eds. *The L=A=N=G=U=A=G=E Book*. Carbondale: Southern Illinois University Press, 1984.

Antin, David. *What It Means to Be Avant-Garde*. New York: New Directions, 1993.

Artaud, Antonin. *The Theater and Its Double*. Translated by Mary Caroline Richards. New York: Grove Press, 1958.

Auden, W. H. "Caliban to the Audience." In *The Selected Poetry of W. H. Auden*. New York: Modern Library, 1958.

Bakhtin, M. M. *The Dialogic Imagination: Four Essays*. Translated by Caryl Emerson and Michael Holquist. Austin: University of Texas Press, 1981.

Bataille, Georges. "The Notion of Expenditure." In *Visions of Excess: Selected Writings, 1927–1939*, translated by Allan Stoekl. Minneapolis: University of Minnesota Press, 1985.

Beach, Christopher, ed. *Artifice and Indeterminacy: An Anthology of New Poetics*. Tuscaloosa: University of Alabama Press, 1998.

Bell, Marvin. *The Book of the Dead Man*. Port Townsend, Wash.: Copper Canyon Press, 1994.

Bernstein, Charles. "Artifice of Absorption." In *A Poetics*. Cambridge, Mass.: Harvard University Press, 1992.

————. *Content's Dream: Essays, 1975–1984*. Los Angeles: Sun and Moon Press, 1986.

————. *Dark City*. Los Angeles: Sun and Moon Press, 1994.

————. *My Way: Speeches and Poems*. Chicago: University of Chicago Press, 1999.

————. *Republics of Reality, 1975–1995*. Los Angeles: Sun and Moon Press, 2000.

————, ed. *Close Listening: Poetry and the Performed Word*. New York: Oxford University Press, 1998.

————, ed. *43 Poets (1984)*. Special issue of *Boundary 2* 14, nos. 1–2 (1985/86).

Blanchot, Maurice. "The Language of Fiction." In *The Work of Fire*, translated by Charlotte Mandell. Stanford, Calif.: Stanford University Press, 1995.

Brown, Bill. *A Sense of Things: The Object Matter of American Literature*. Chicago: University of Chicago Press, 2003.

Bruns, Gerald L. "The Concepts of Art and Poetry in Emmanuel Levinas's Writings." In *The Cambridge Companion to Levinas*, edited by Simon Critchley and Robert Bernasconi. Cambridge, Mass.: Cambridge University Press, 2002.

————. "Donald Davidson among the Outcasts." In *Tragic Thoughts at the End of Philosophy: Language, Literature, and Ethical Theory*. Evanston, Ill.: Northwestern University Press, 1999.

————. *Maurice Blanchot: The Refusal of Philosophy*. Baltimore: Johns Hopkins University Press, 1997.

————. *Modern Poetry and the Idea of Language: A Critical and Historical Study*. New Haven, Conn.: Yale University Press, 1974.

————. "Towards a Hermeneutics of Freedom." In *Hermeneutics Ancient and Modern*. New Haven, Conn.: Yale University Press, 1992.

Burns, Gerald. *Shorter Poems*. Normal, Ill.: Dalkey Archive Press, 1993.

————. "The Slate Notebook." In *Toward a Phenomenology of Written Art*. New Paltz, N.Y.: Treacle Press, 1979.

————. *A Thing about Language*. Carbondale: Southern Illinois University Press, 1990.

Cage, John. *Silence*. Middletown, Conn.: Wesleyan University Press, 1961.

Cavell, Stanley. *Disowning Knowledge in Six Plays of Shakespeare*. Cambridge, Mass.: Cambridge University Press, 1987.

————. *The Senses of Walden: An Expanded Edition*. San Francisco: North Point Press, 1981.

Cayley, John. "Hypertext/Cybertext/Poetext." In *Assembling Alternatives: Reading Postmodern Poetries Transnationally*, edited by Romana Huk. Middletown, Conn.: Wesleyan University Press, 2003.

Celan, Paul. *Dritter Band*. Vol. 3 of *Gesammelte Werke*. Frankfurt: Suhrkamp Verlag, 1983.

Chopin, Henri. "Why I Am the Author of Free and Sound Poetry." Available at UbuWeb (www.ubuweb.com/papers/chopin.html). Accessed May 28, 2004.

Coolidge, Clark. *The Maintains*. Berkeley, Calif.: This Press, 1974.

———. *Talking Poetics from Naropa Institute*. Boulder, Colo.: Shambhala Press, 1978.

Cory, Mark E. "Soundplay: The Polyphonous Tradition of German Radio Art." In Kahn and Whitehead, eds., *Wireless Imagination*.

Crane, Hart. "General Aims and Theories." In *The Complete Poems of Hart Crane*. Garden City, N.Y.: Anchor Books, 1966.

Creeley, Robert. *Was That a Real Poem and Other Essays*. Bolinas, Calif.: Four Seasons Foundation, 1979.

Culler, Jonathan. "Comparing Poetry." *Comparative Literature* 53, no. 3 (2001), vii–xviii.

Danto, Arthur. "The Artworld." *Journal of Philosophy* 61, no. 19 (1964), 571–84.

———. *The Philosophical Disenfranchisement of Art*. New York: Columbia University Press, 1986.

———. *The Transfiguration of the Commonplace: A Philosophy of Art*. Cambridge, Mass.: Harvard University Press, 1981.

Davidson, Donald. "A Nice Derangement of Epitaphs." In *Philosophical Grounds of Rationality: Intentions, Categories, Ends*, edited by Richard E. Grandy and Richard Warner. Oxford: Clarendon Press, 1986.

Davidson, Michael. *Ghostlier Demarcations: Modern Poetry and the Material World*. Berkeley: University of California Press, 1997.

Debord, Guy. "All the King's Men." In *The Situationist Anthology*, edited and translated by Ken Knabb. Berkeley, Calif.: Bureau of Public Secrets, 1981.

Deleuze, Gilles, and Felix Guattari. *A Thousand Plateaus: Capitalism and Schizophrenia*. Translated by Brian Massumi. Minneapolis: University of Minnesota Press, 1987.

Derrida, Jacques. "Proverb: 'He That Would Pun. . . .'" In *GLASsery*, edited by John P. Leavey Jr. Lincoln: University of Nebraska Press, 1987.

Drucker, Johanna. *The Visible Word: Experimental Typography and Modern Art, 1909–1925*. Chicago: University of Chicago Press, 1994.

————. "Visual Performance of the Poetic Text." In Bernstein, ed., *Close Listening*.

DuPlessis, Rachel Blau. *The Pink Guitar*. New York: Routledge, 1990.

Dworkin, Craig. *Reading the Illegible*. Evanston, Ill.: Northwestern University Press, 2003.

Fisher, Allen. "The Poetics of the Complexity Manifold." In *99 Poets / 1999: An International Poetics Symposium*, edited by Charles Bernstein. Special issue of *Boundary 2* 26, no. 1 (1999), 115–18.

Foucault, Michel. "The Abnormals." In *The Essential Works of Foucault*, vol. 1, *Ethics and Subjectivity*, edited by Paul Rabinow. New York: New Press, 1997.

————. "Discourse on Language." Translated by Rupert Swyer. In *The Archeology of Knowledge*, translated by A. M. Sheridan Smith. New York: Pantheon Books, 1972.

————. "On the Genealogy of Ethics: An Overview of Work in Progress." In *Ethics: Subjectivity and Truth*, translated by Robert Hurley et al. New York: New Press, 1997.

————. *L'Ordre du discours* (Paris: Editions Gallimard, 1971).

————. "Truth and Power." In *The Essential Works of Foucault*, vol. 3, *Power*, edited by James D. Faubion. New York: New Press, 1997.

Fredman, Stephen. *A Minora for Athena: Charles Resnikoff and the Jewish Dilemmas of Objectivist Poetry*. Chicago: University of Chicago Press, 2001.

————. *Poet's Prose: The Crisis in American Verse*. 2nd ed. Cambridge, Mass.: Cambridge University Press, 1992.

Gadamer, Hans-Georg. *Truth and Method*. 2nd ed. Translated by Joel Weinsheimer and Donald G. Marshall. New York: Crossroad Publishing, 1989.

Gavronsky, Serge. "Interview with Francis Ponge." In *Poems and Texts*, translated by Serge Gavronsky. New York: October House, 1969.

Gomringer, Eugen. "From Line to Constellation." In *Concrete Poetry: A World View*, edited by Mary Ellen Solt. Bloomington: Indiana University Press, 1969.

Graham, Dan. *"Schema March 1966." Art-Language* 1, no. 1 (1969), 14.

Graham, Jorie. *Materialism*. Hopewell, N.J.: Ecco Press, 1993.

Habermas, Jürgen. "Philosophy as Stand-in and Interpreter." In *Moral Consciousness and Communicative Action*, translated by Christian Lenhardt and Shierry Weber Nicholson. Cambridge, Mass.: MIT Press, 1990.

Havelock, Eric. *Preface to Plato*. Cambridge, Mass.: Harvard University Press, 1963.

Hayles, N. Katherine. *Writing Machines*. Cambridge, Mass.: MIT Press, 2002.

Heidegger, Martin. *Being and Time*. Translated by John Macquarrie and Edward Robinson. New York: Harper and Row, 1962.

Hejinian, Lyn. *The Language of Inquiry*. Berkeley: University of California Press, 2000.

—————. *Writing as an Aid to Memory*. Los Angeles: Sun and Moon Press, 1996.

Higgins, Dick. *Modernism since Postmodernism: Essays on Intermedia*. San Diego: San Diego State University Press, 1997.

Ikonen, Teemu. "Moving Text in Avant-Garde Poetry: Towards a Poetics of Textual Motion." *Dichtung-digital.de Newsletter* 4 (2003), edited by Marku Eskelinen. Available at dichtung-digital (http://www.dichtung-digital.de/2003/4-ikonen.htm). Accessed May 28, 2004.

Jameson, Fredric. *Late Marxism: Adorno, or, The Persistence of the Dialectic*. London: Verso, 1990.

—————. *Postmodernism: or, the Cultural Logic of Late Capitalism*. Durham, N.C.: Duke University Press, 1991.

Kac, Eduardo. "Holopoetry, Hypertext, Hyperpoetry." In *Holographic Imaging and Materials*, edited by Tung H. Jeong. Bellingham, Wash.: SPIE, 1993.

Kahn, Douglas. *Noise, Water, Meat: A History of Sound in the Arts*. Cambridge, Mass.: MIT Press, 1999.

Kahn, Douglas, and Gregory Whitehead, eds. *Wireless Imagination: Sound, Radio, and the Avant-Garde*. Cambridge, Mass.: MIT Press, 1992.

Kenner, Hugh. *The Poetry of Ezra Pound*. London: Faber and Faber, 1951.

—————. *The Pound Era*. Berkeley: University of California Press, 1971.

—————. "Pound Typing." In *The Mechanic Muse*. New York: Oxford University Press, 1987.

—————. *The Stoic Comedians: Flaubert, Joyce, and Beckett*. Berkeley: University of California Press, 1974.

Kittler, Friedrich. *Gramophone, Film, Typewriter*. Translated by Geoffrey Winthrop-Young and Michael Wutz. Stanford, Calif.: Stanford University Press, 1999.

Kostelanetz, Richard, ed. *Text-Sound Texts*. New York: William Morrow, 1980.

Kristeva, Julia. "Pour une sémiologie des paragrammes." In *Εημειωτιχη: Recherchés pour une sémanalyse*. Paris: Seuil, 1969.

Langbaum, Robert. *The Poetry of Experience: The Dramatic Monologue in Modern Tradition*. New York: W. W. Norton, 1956.

Leggott, Michelle J. *Reading Zukofsky's 80 Flowers*. Baltimore: Johns Hopkins University Press, 1989.

Levarie, Siegmund. "Noise." *Critical Inquiry* 4, no. 1 (1977), 21–31.

Levinas, Emmanuel. "Language and Proximity." In *Collected Philosophical Papers*, translated by Alphonso Lingis. The Hague: Martinus Nijhoff, 1987.

———. *The Levinas Reader*. Edited by Séan Hand. Oxford: Basil Blackwell, 1989.

———. *Otherwise than Being, or Beyond Essence*. Translated by Alphonso Lingis. The Hague: Martinus Nijhoff, 1981.

Lyotard, Jean-François. "La dent, la paume." In *Des dispositifs pulsionels*. Paris: UGE, 1973.

Mac Cormack, Karen. *At Issue*. Toronto: Coach House Books, 2001.

———. *Quill Driver*. Toronto: Nightwood Editions, 1989.

MacIntyre, Alasdair. *After Virtue: A Study in Moral Theory*. Notre Dame, Ind.: University of Notre Dame Press, 1981.

———. *Three Rival Versions of Moral Inquiry: Encyclopedia, Genealogy, and Tradition*. Notre Dame, Ind.: University of Notre Dame Press, 1990.

———. *Whose Justice? Which Rationality?* Notre Dame, Ind.: University of Notre Dame Press, 1989.

Mac Low, Jackson. *Representative Works, 1938–1985*. New York: ROOF Books, 1986.

Mallarmé, Stéphane. "The Book, a Spiritual Instrument." In *Mallarmé: Selected Prose Poems, Essays, and Letters*, translated by Bradford Cook. Baltimore: Johns Hopkins University Press, 1956.

Marion, Jean-Luc. *The Crossing of the Visible*. Translated by James K. A. Smith. Stanford, Calif.: Stanford University Press, 2004.

———. *In Excess: Studies of Saturated Phenomena*. New York: Fordham University Press, 2001.

McCaffery, Steve. *Carnival: The Second Panel, 1970–75*. Toronto: Coach House Books, n.d.

———. "Discussion . . . Genesis . . . Continuity: Some Reflections in the Current Work of the Four Horsemen." In Kostelanetz, ed., *Text-Sound Texts*.

———. *North of Intention: Critical Writings, 1976–1982*. New York: ROOF Books, 1986.

———. *Prior to Meaning: The Protosemantic and Poetics*. Evanston, Ill.: Northwestern University Press, 2001.

————. *Seven Pages Missing.* Vol. 1, *Selected Texts, 1969–2000.* Toronto: Coach House Books, 2000.

————. *Seven Pages Missing.* Vol 2, *Previously Uncollected Texts, 1968–2000.* Toronto: Coach House Books, 2002.

McCaffery, Steve, and bp Nichol. "Report 2: Narrative." In *Rational Geomancy: The Collected Research Reports of the Toronto Research Group, 1973–1982.* Vancouver, B.C.: Talonbooks, 1992.

————, eds. *Sound Poetry: A Catalogue.* Toronto: Underwhich Editions, 1978.

McCorkle, James, ed. *Conversant Essays: Contemporary Poets on Poetry.* Detroit: Wayne State University Press, 1990.

McGann, Jerome. *Black Riders: The Visible Language of Modernism.* Princeton, N.J.: Princeton University Press, 1993.

Messerli, Douglas, ed. *Language Poetries.* New York: New Directions, 1986.

Milosz, Czeslaw. *The Captive Mind.* Translated by Jane Zielonko. New York: Vintage Books, 1981.

Morris, Adalaide, ed. *Sound States: Innovative Poetics and Acoustical Technologies.* Chapel Hill: University of North Carolina Press, 1997.

Novarina, Valère. *The Theater of the Ears.* Translated by Allen S. Weiss. Los Angeles: Sun and Moon Press, 1996.

Nussbaum, Martha. "Flawed Crystals: *The Golden Bowl* as Moral Philosophy." In *Love's Knowledge: Essays on Literature and Philosophy.* New York: Oxford University Press, 1990.

Olson, Charles. "Projective Verse." In *The Human Universe and Other Essays,* edited by Donald Allen. New York: Grove Press, 1967.

Olson, Elder. "Outline of Poetic Theory." In *Critics and Criticism: Ancient and Modern,* edited by R. S. Crane. Chicago: University of Chicago Press, 1952.

Ong, Walter J., S.J. "System, Space, and Intellect in Renaissance Symbolism." In *The Barbarian Within, and Other Fugitive Essays.* New York: MacMillan, 1962.

Orange, Tom. "Notes for a Reading of *Ace.*" *Removed for Further Study: The Poetry of Tom Raworth.* Special issue of *The Gig* 13–14 (May 2003), 161–69.

Palmer, Michael. "On Objectivism." *Sulfur* 10, no. 1 (1990), 117–26.

————, ed. *Code of Signals: Recent Writings in Poetics.* Berkeley, Calif.: North Atlantic Books, 1983.

Perelman, Bob. "The Marginalization of Poetry." In *The Marginalization of Poetry: Language Writing and Literary History.* Princeton, N.J.: Princeton University Press, 1996.

Perloff, Marjorie. " 'Concrete Prose': Haroldo de Campos; *Galáxias* and After." *Contemporary Literature* 42, no. 2 (2001), 270–93.

———. *The Dance of the Intellect: Studies in the Poetry of the Pound Tradition.* Cambridge, Mass.: Cambridge University Press, 1986.

———. "Language Poetry and the Lyric Subject: Susan Howe's Buffalo, Ron Silliman's Albany." *Critical Inquiry* 25 (spring 1999), 405–34.

———. *Poetry on and off the Page: Essays for Emergent Occasions.* Evanston, Ill.: Northwestern University Press, 1998.

———. *Twenty-first-Century Modernism: The "New" Poetics.* Oxford: Basil Blackwell, 2002.

Ponge, Francis. *The Making of the* Pré. Translated by Lee Fahnestock. Columbia: University of Missouri Press, 1979.

———. *Le parti pris des choses, suive de Proêmes.* Paris: Gallimard, 1948.

———. *The Power of Language: Texts and Translations.* Translated by Serge Gavronsky. Berkeley: University of California Press, 1979.

———. *Selected Poems.* Translated by C. K. Williams, John Montague, and Margaret Guiton. Winston-Salem, N.C.: Wake Forest University Press, 1994.

Pound, Ezra. *The Literary Essays of Ezra Pound.* Edited by T. S. Eliot. London: Faber and Faber, 1954.

———. *The Pisan Cantos.* New York: New Directions, 1948.

———. *Selected Poems.* New York: New Directions, 1957.

Quartermain, Peter. *Disjunctive Poetics: From Gertrude Stein and Zukofsky to Susan Howe.* Cambridge, Mass.: Cambridge University Press, 1992.

Rasula, Jed, and Steve McCaffery, eds. *Imagining Language.* Cambridge, Mass.: MIT Press, 1998.

Rauschenberg, Robert. Interview by Deborah Solomon. *New York Times Magazine,* February 15, 2004, 13.

Retallack, Joan. *Afterrimages.* Hanover, N.H.: Wesleyan University Press, 1995.

———. *How to Do Things with Words.* Los Angeles: Sun and Moon Press, 1998.

Rorty, Richard. "Heidegger, Kundera, and Dickens." In *Essays on Heidegger and Others.* Cambridge, Mass.: Cambridge University Press, 1991.

Sharp, Willoughby. "Lawrence Weiner at Amsterdam." *Avalanche* 4 (spring 1972).

Silliman, Ron. "Disappearance of the Word, Appearance of the World." In Andrews and Bernstein, eds., *The L=A=N=G=U=A=G=E Book.*

———. *The New Sentence.* New York: ROOF Books, 1987.

————, ed. *In the American Tree: Language, Realism, Poetry.* Orono, Maine: National Poetry Foundation, 1986.

Simic, Charles. *Dime-Store Alchemy: The Art of Joseph Cornell.* Hopewell, N.J.: Ecco Press, 1992.

————. *The Metaphysician in the Dark.* Ann Arbor: University of Michigan Press, 2003.

Solt, Mary Ellen, ed. *Concrete Poetry: A World View.* Bloomington: Indiana University Press, 1968.

Spicer, Jack. "After Lorca." In *The Collected Books of Jack Spicer,* edited by Robin Blaser. Santa Rosa, Calif.: Black Sparrow Press, 1989.

Stein, Gertrude. *Writings and Lectures, 1909–1945.* Edited by Patricia Meyerowitz. Hammondsworth, England: Penguin Books, 1971.

Strand, Mark. *The Continuous Life.* New York: Alfred A. Knopf, 1999.

Strauss, David Lee. "Approaching *80 Flowers.*" In Palmer, ed., *Code of Signals.*

Strauss, Leo. *Persecution and the Art of Writing.* Glencoe, Ill.: Free Press, 1952.

Travis, Tim. "Strange Attraction: Our Lady of Found Objects." *Things Magazine: New Writing about Objects* 15 (winter 2001–2), 60–70.

Waldenfels, Bernard. "The Ruled and the Unruly: Functions and Limits of Institutional Regulations." In *The Public Realm: Essays on Discursive Types in Political Philosophy,* edited by Rainer Schürmann. Albany: SUNY Press, 1989.

Waldrop, Rosemarie. "Form and Discontent." *Diacritics: A Review of Contemporary Criticism,* nos. 3–4 (fall–winter 1996), 54–62.

Wallace, Mark, and Steven Marks, eds. *Telling It Slant: Avant-Garde Poetics of the 1990s.* Tuscaloosa: University of Alabama Press, 2002.

Watten, Barrett. "Total Syntax: The Work in the World." In Beach, ed., *Artifice and Indeterminacy.*

Williams, Emmett, ed. *An Anthology of Concrete Poetry.* New York: Something Else Press, 1967.

Williams, William Carlos. *Imaginations.* Edited by Webster Schott. New York: New Directions, 1970.

————. "Pastoral." In *Selected Poems,* edited by Charles Tomlinson. New York: New Directions, 1985.

————. *Paterson.* New York: New Directions, 1963.

Wittgenstein, Ludwig. *Philosophical Investigations.* Translated by G. E. M. Anscombe. Cambridge, Mass.: Cambridge University Press, 1953.

Ziarek, Krzysztof. "Word for Sign: Poetic Language in Coolidge's *The Crystal Text*." *Sagetrieb* 10, nos. 1–2 (1991), 145–66.

Zukofsky, Louis. *Complete Short Poetry*. Baltimore: Johns Hopkins University Press, 1991.

———. *Prepositions+: The Collected Critical Essays*. Edited by Mark Scroggins. Hanover, N.H.: Wesleyan University Press, 2000.

———. *A Test of Poetry*. Hanover, N.H.: Wesleyan University Press, 2000.

Index